THINKING MAKING

A WITHERING LACK OF IMAGINATION CRIPPLES THE ADVANCEMENT OF MODERN CULTURE. COMPLACENCY AND NARROWMINDEDNESS SUPPORT THE QUICKENING CREEP OF SOCIAL-POLITICAL REACTION AND OUR DIMMING VISION OF HUMAN PROGRESS. THE FASHIONABLE COMMENTARY OF MODEST DECLINE AND CULTURAL RETRENCHMENT BORES SOCIETY TO DEATH. NOTHING SUBSTANTIAL HAPPENS BEYOND THE INCREASINGLY FREQUENT CRASH OF UNTENABLE POWER STRUCTURES AND THE MINDLESS SCURRYING TO REPAINT THE SAME OR EVEN OLDER PICTURES OVER THE YAWNING GAPS. THE INTELLECTUAL LEADERSHIP THAT ONCE CHAMPIONED A BRAVE NEW WORLD OF THE HUMAN SPIRIT—ACHIEVED THROUGH STUNNING ADVANCES IN SCIENCE, ART, AND TECHNOLOGY—ABANDONS THIS EXCITING AND COURAGEOUS VISION AND PROCLAIMS A NEW AGE OF CONSERVATISM, MODESTY, AND RESIGNATION. AT BEST WE ARE OFFERED CULTURAL STAGNATION, AT WORST THE SYSTEMATIC DISMANTLING OF THE HEROIC PROGRESS OF MODERN THOUGHT AND ACTION. FROM THE INTELLECTUAL HEAVENS A DENSE FOG OF FATUOUS WORDS AND SPECIOUS IMAGES DRIZZLES DOWN ON THE DEEPENING MUD OF OUR WORLD'S PRODUCTIVE IMAGINATION. ART RETREATS FROM AN ACTIVE ROLE IN THE MAKING OF THE MATERIAL WORLD AND THE ORCHESTRATION OF HUMAN RELATIONSHIPS AND FOUNDERS AS A PERIPHERAL ACTIVITY. IT SINKS INTO AN IMPOTENT CRITICAL ROLE, ACCEPTABLE TO AND EVEN SUPPORTIVE OF AN INEQUITABLE SOCIAL HIERARCHY, AS A NAUGHTY YET INEFFECTUAL OPPOSITION. FLAT PSEUDO-INTELLECTUAL CRITICISM AND CYNICAL, SUPERFICIAL, VACUOUSLY APOCALYPTIC PATHOS SURRENDER THE TRADITIONAL POWER ART WIELDS IN THE CONSTRUCTION OF THE WORLD, ITS LIFE, AND IDEAS. THE POWER OF THE MATERIAL ARTS RESIDES LESS IN THEIR CAPACITY TO MAKE CRITICISM, THAN IN THE POTENTIAL TO CHANGE THE WORLD IN SUPPORT OF NEW IDEAS, NEW STRUCTURES. ART THAT CRITICIZES ACQUIRES ONLY AN IMAGE OF POLITICAL OPPOSITION, WHILE ACTUALLY UNDERMINING NOT ONLY THE MATERIAL SIGNIFICANCE OF THE WORK BUT ALSO ITS CAPACITY TO ACHIEVE A REAL POLITICAL SIGNIFICANCE IN EFFECTING PHYSICAL CHANGES IN THE WORLD. A GENUINE, POLITICAL ART RESISTS THE CONCEPTUAL IN FAVOR OF THE MATERIAL. THERE IS NO TIME FOR ART TO SPLASH QUIETLY ABOUT IN CLEVER COMMENTARY AND CYNICAL DISSIPATION—REACTION UNSELECTIVELY TEARS DOWN THE MODERN WORLD AND ITS FUTURE (WITH THE SLOGAN "IT DIDN'T WORK") FASTER THAN ANYONE IS NOW IMAGINING AND BUILDING THE CONTINUAL EXPANSION OF HUMAN POSSIBILITIES. ART MUST TAKE A LESS CYNICAL ATTITUDE TOWARD MATERIAL CHANGE. EVERYWHERE THERE IS THE NEED AND OPPORTUNITY TO DREAM UP AND START MAKING WHOLE NEW WORLDS AGAIN.

FIRST PUBLISHED IN
HARVARD ARCHITECTURE REVIEW 7, 1986.

When my new truck rolled over the first thing I did was jump out fast like if I didn't I maybe wouldn't. I looked back at the whole thing from far away, all my tools stringing out from the burst-open job-box, its flaps stuck up like a jerky little bird. It was early morning, sunny and cold and almost wonderful to see all this great stuff laid out in front of me: a condensed history of every two-bit project we'd ever dreamed our lives around. Heavy-duty power tools and a beat-up truck. That was the beginning of my first serious thinking about body shops since Peter and I had pulled dents for cash in high school. This country is crawling with body shops—there must be 50 or 100 on Pacific Avenue alone, all underutilized and waiting for someone to walk in and say, "OK, today we're gonna make some candy apple, bent-metal, chopped and channeled stuff that isn't a car." And body shops aren't all. It's like the wreckers in Houston. Even if they had let us drive the crane in over the lawn we never could have swung that thing up the side of the parking garage as slick as we did towing it up with two flashing-light wreckers on the roof. And they were really into it. Ordinary, everyday life and work in this country is just waiting for someone to put some imagination behind it, to make the whole world a little different or even better. What we're going to do is buy a great big rusting hulk of an old ship named the Jet Maru, full of tall cranes and diesel winches like we saw them cutting up in Tacoma, and set up a huge off-shore metal shop. We'll build all kinds of things that they probably haven't seen on the land before and tow it around the world with an oceangoing tug. We'll unload stuff on barges whenever we finish, except for the floating pieces that we can just cut loose. What we really need for this kind of work is one of those great big Sikorsky sky cranes like they use for logging and fighting wars so we could just grab a hold of something really big and fly it somewhere where people want to have it. The whole operation is mobile. The important vehicles are the flatbed semis so everything can travel easily, but we'll need to carry along a cat, at least a D6, and a light crane. Concrete we'll order from near the site, but everything else we'll bring along, except for the stuff that people have built there before us. We already have most of the trucks and tools we need. Do you know that there's a whole desert of mothballed 747s that they could let us use? And once they have all the B-1s, there's no reason why we couldn't have the B-52s, and when they have the Stealths we can have the B-1s, and we could probably have the space shuttle right now. We could do a lot of the preliminary site work with the bombers and then fly in a C-130 transport with short runway capability. The nose drops and the three of us come blasting out in a jeep. Cam's dri_____ _____ sitting on the seatback with a walkie-talkie. Mar__ _____ ne through binoculars as fat yello_____ __rs and the terrorists understa___ _____ ures are behind us now. We'r_

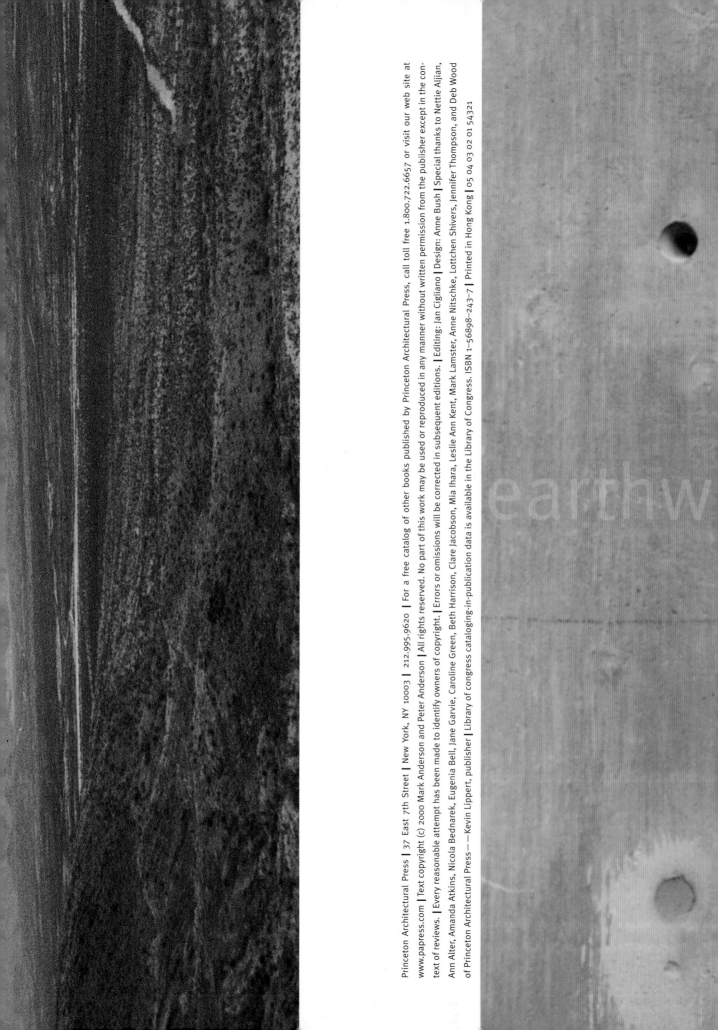

Princeton Architectural Press | 37 East 7th Street | New York, NY 10003 | 212.995.9620 | For a free catalog of other books published by Princeton Architectural Press, call toll free 1.800.722.6657 or visit our web site at www.papress.com | Text copyright (c) 2000 Mark Anderson and Peter Anderson | All rights reserved. No part of this work may be used or reproduced in any manner without written permission from the publisher except in the context of reviews. | Every reasonable attempt has been made to identify owners of copyright. | Errors or omissions will be corrected in subsequent editions. | Editing: Jan Cigliano | Design: Anne Bush | Special thanks to Nettie Aljian, Ann Alter, Amanda Atkins, Nicola Bednarek, Eugenia Bell, Jane Garvie, Caroline Green, Beth Harrison, Clare Jacobson, Mia Ihara, Leslie Ann Kent, Mark Lamster, Anne Nitschke, Lottchen Shivers, Jennifer Thompson, and Deb Wood of Princeton Architectural Press——Kevin Lippert, publisher | Library of congress cataloging-in-publication data is available in the Library of Congress. ISBN 1-56898-243-7 | Printed in Hong Kong | 05 04 03 02 01 54321

INTRODUCTION BY
Donlyn Lyndon

TEXT AND PROJECTS BY
Mark Anderson
Peter Anderson

INCLUDING PROJECT COLLABORATIONS WITH
Cameron Schoepp
Andrew Zago

k.framing.plumbing.

ANDERSON ANDERSON
ARCHITECTURE AND CONSTRUCTION

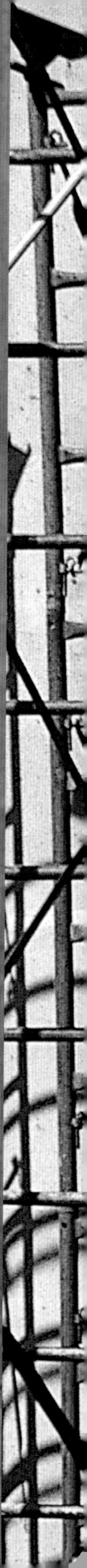

Princeton Architectural Press
New York 2000

INTRODUCTION BY DONLYN LYNDON 10
EARTHWORK. FRAMING. PLUMBING. 12
MAKING THINGS 13

EARTHWORK 16
LANDSCAPES 18
STEEP HILLS AND WATERFRONT 28
WARPING TO THE SITE 38
SAGGING ROOFS AND DROOPING FLOORS 50

FRAMING 68
AFFORDABLE PREFABRICATION 76
ECONOMICS, GLU-LAMS, AND SOCIAL CHANGE 90
HYBRID FRAMING 100
PUBLIC IMAGINATION 118

PLUMBING 130
LIQUID SPACE 132
CLOUDS AND FULLNESS 146
LIVE FILM 166
AMBİENT INFRASTRUCTURE 174

•
PROJECT LIST 184
ACKNOWLEDGMENTS 188
DESIGN AND CONSTRUCTION TEAM 190
PHOTO CREDITS 191
BIOGRAPHIES 192

CONTENTS

This book is organized and indexed using a standardized North American system of numbers and titles, a system that is widely used to sequentially order construction information. Developed by the Construction Specifications Institute (CSI) and Construction Specifications Canada (CSC), this index system is the standard format used by architects, contractors, and suppliers in organizing and cross-referencing construction drawings, written specifications, reference materials, and legal documents. Having once resisted its seemingly authoritarian and limiting categories, we have begun to think that there may be some creative potential in working with this standard code.

CSI INDEX

KEY TO INDEX NUMBERS:
—**REFERENCE NOTED IN TEXT**
—**(GENERAL REFERENCE TO INFORMATION ON PAGE)**
—REFERENCE TO IMAGE

EXISTING CONDITIONS
PROJECT FINANCIAL INFORMATION

JOB SITE ADMINISTRATION
FIELD ENGINEERING
REGULATORY REQUIREMENTS
REFERENCE STANDARDS
PROJECT MEETINGS
MATERIAL DELIVERY, STORAGE, AND HANDLING

SUBSURFACE INVESTIGATION
SELECTIVE DEMOLITION
SITE PREPARATION
EARTHWORK
LANDSCAPE

STRUCTURAL METAL FRAMING
METAL FABRICATIONS
EXPANSION CONTROL

FASTENERS AND ADHESIVES
FRAMING
STRUCTURAL PANELS
PREFABRICATED STRUCTURAL WOOD
FINISH CARPENTRY
PLASTIC FABRICATIONS

PREPARED ROLL ROOFING

WINDOWS AND DOORS

PAINTING

AUDIO-VISUAL RECORDING/PROJECTION
OBSERVATORY EQUIPMENT

AIR SUPPORTED STRUCTURES
INTEGRATED ASSEMBLIES
PRE-ENGINEERED STRUCTURES
RECORDING INSTRUMENTATION
SOLAR ENERGY AND ILLUMINATION

SCAFFOLDING AND PLATFORMS
PEOPLE MOVER SYSTEMS
PLUMBING
STEAM AND STEAM CONDENSATE
HEAT GENERATION AND TRANSFER

COMMUNICATIONS

00230   8, 29, **31**, **34**, 38, **45**, **(51)**, 55, 56, **66**, **71**, **73**, **79**, **(91)**, **95**, **104**, **106**, **117**, **123**, **135**, **(142)**, 148, **(149)**, **156**, 160

00240   **21**, **31**, **34**, **(51)**, **71**, **73**, **78**, **85**, **86**, **87**, **95**, **96**, **97**, **106**, **120**, **(142)**, **(172)**, **178**, **179**

01043   **12**, **14**, **(29)**, **34**, **35**, **44**, **73**, **79**, **86**, **88**, 89, **96**, **97**, 98, **(133)**, **178**, **179**, **(180)**

01050   **21**, **31**, **34**, **35**, 47, **72**, **73**, **86**, **106**, 137, **(180)**

01060   **13**, **54**, 55, **66**, 77, **79**, **95**, **96**, **97**

01091   **(5)**, **14**, **34**, **72**, **(77)**, 77, **79**, **86**, **88**, **106**, **121**, **(152)**, **178**, **(180)**

01200   **(119)**, **120**, **121**, **123**, **179**, **(180)**

01600   **71**, **74**, 76, **85**, **87**, 87, 89, **97**, 102, **(133)**

02010   **12**, **14**, **21**, 21, 33, **35**, **88**, 98, **(142)**, 145, 146, 150, 160, **(180)**

02070   **34**, **35**, **45**, **73**, **74**, **117**, **120**

02100   **34**, **35**, 40, **54**, **85**, **120**, **121**

02200   **12**, **17**, **71**, **74**, **85**, **(127)**, 130, **(142)**, 144, 171

02900   18, **(19)**, **(29)**, **31**, **34**, 43, **45**, 50, **54**, **61**, 67, **67**, **71**, **78**, **95**, **117**, **123**, 124, **(127)**, **(129)**, **(142)**, 154, 175, **(180)**

05100   **61**, **97**, **(101)**, **104**, 109, **117**, **(129)**

05500   46, **72**, **73**, 93, 114, **117**, **(129)**, **135**, **169**, 170, 171, 192

05800   82, **85**, **86**, **95**

06050   **79**, 82, **(133)**, 140

06100   **13**, **44**, **66**, **69**, **75**, **(77)**, **78**, 83, **85**, **87**, 98, **(101)**, **106**

06120   **54**, **61**, 64, **(101)**, **104**

06170   **54**, **(77)**, **86**, **87**, 93, 94, 100, 103, **104**, 107

06200   **(29)**, 30, 41, **44**, **45**, 48, 85, **86**, **104**, **106**

06600   23, **135**, 136, **(143)**, 166, **169**, 170

07520   **79**, 82, **86**

08000   **44**, **61**, **66**, 84, **86**, **97**, **(101)**, **104**, 106, **120**, **121**, **123**, **(127)**, **(143)**, 160, **162**, **(180)**, 182

09990   41, **45**, 48, **61**, **73**, **(152)**, **179**

11130   **14**, **22**, **74**, **75**, **117**, **120**, **121**, 128, 157, **162**, 164, **169**, 169, 175, 176, **(180)**

11660   18, 20, **22**, 26, 27, **35**, **61**, **66**, **104**, **110**, 110, 116, 117, 122, **123**, **135**, 145, **162**, **(180)**, 192

13010   **14**, 70, **75**, **86**, **(133)**, 137, **(143)**, **169**

13020   **15**, 89, 93, **97**, **(101)**, **104**, 109, 110, **(119)**, **(129)**, **(153)**, **169**, 179, **(180)**

13120   **78**, **79**, 80, 83, 89, 93, 94, **95**, **96**, **97**, 97

13500   134, **(143)**, **(153)**, **156**, 159, **162**, **169**, 169, **(172)**, **(173)**, **(180)**

13600   **31**, 37, **45**, **54**, **61**, 62, **66**, **67**, **72**, **95**, **104**, **110**, 111, **117**, 132, **135**, 137, **(143)**, **162**, **169**, **(180)**

14800   **21**, **22**, 24, **123**, 126, **(129)**, **(143)**, **(153)**, **169**, **(180)**

14910   **22**, 24, **74**, **(143)**, **178**, **(180)**, 182

15400   **14**, **15**, 68, **71**, **74**, **75**, **123**, **(127)**, **131**, **135**, 138, **156**, **162**, 166, **169**, **(180)**

15525   **35**, **123**, **(127)**, **(129)**, **(142)**, **(143)**, **(173)**

15550   **35**, **(129)**, 132, **135**, **(142)**, **(143)**, **169**, **(173)**, 175, **(180)**

16700   **15**, **162**, 164, **(172)**, **178**, 179, **(180)**

Clouds: Mark and Peter Anderson talk a lot about clouds. Not the classic sort of cloud, big and sculptural and tinted picturesquely, not the clouds of Le Corbusier's Hellenic landscapes or Utzon's hovering forms that illustrate Platforms and Plateaus: Ideas of a Danish Architect, but something more northwestern . . . something more like mists and fog, or more timely . . . like neurons.

Clouds don't fit very well in the organizational scheme adopted for this book, which is borrowed from the Construction Specifications Institute's categories of Earthwork, Framing and Plumbing; but never mind, the ambitions of the authors are much more spacious than the pragmatic subtitle *Architecture and Construction* suggests.

Anderson Anderson present us with a skyful of projects, anecdotes, suggestions, and pronouncements. What's exhilarating about this book is the way in which their intentions seep into an array of differing kinds of communication: job notes and correspondence; place descriptions; art installations designed to evoke the atmosphere and engage the body; computer images and project photos; construction documents and illustrations; as well as rhetorical pronouncements. The whole is saturated with a sense of the architectural adventure.

The projects, too, are varied and surprising, ranging from well crafted and imaginative extensions of the wooden architecture of the Northwest United States to provocative emulation of the mudflats of Anchorage Alaska, tremulous observation towers in the plains of Texas, and on to speculations on the digital age (posing as competition entries). There are also many stops in Japan. . .to bring American stick building technology, based on 2x4 Western platform framing, to the land that is conventionally considered to be the Mecca of fine wood crafting. These folk are not easily confined.

Attitudes have a lot to do with geography. One should not expect people raised in the forests of the Pacific Northwest to seek the bare, sculptural glory of California's rolling and golden hills. Nor would they be likely to have been mesmerized by those scenes of upright classical fragments standing in bold and singular relief against the hills of the Greek horizon that so formed Le Corbusier's young imagination. In Earthwork, Anderson Anderson describe, instead, being amongst the trees and forest undercover: recognizing the throbbing life force of the soil, roots, and vegetable matter; playing in the mud; wending their way through thickets of shrub; glimpsing the sun breaking through the overcast, late in the day, and reflecting across the waters of Puget Sound. Mount Rainier, their region's most famous but oft-shrouded (in clouds) landmark, is for them an elusive and mythic presence—an event, not a landform. External form, they tell us, doesn't really interest them. Their quest is for the experience of being inside and near, with the full body engaged—not outside and picturing (posturing?) with the mind's "disembodied" eye.

They also like to be near the action. They are quintessential "hands-on" architects, having started their practice in design-build, making the places they designed. Though their practice has changed, and their design and conceptualizing activities have widened, they still carry an intellectual tool bag that is used to manipulate "things" and examine how they work. This inventive curiosity makes them sympathetic collaborators for people who like to explore, and the book includes many projects that search beyond the boundaries of expectation.

Their proposal for an elaborate treetop walkway and observation network for the Forest Canopy Study Center at Evergreen State College could only have reached a point of serious consideration with the prodding and support of an adventurous, confident client. The towers and pits exploring a vertical complement to the indefinite reach of the Texas horizon clearly were born and nurtured in the context of an institution with far-reaching goals and intrepid administration. Their sensual installation projects and conceptual proposals have been spurred on by interactions with their frequent collaborator, sculptor Cameron Schoepp, involving spirited consideration of the challenging insights and more diffuse working methods that different disciplines can bring to the work.

Of course, personal, direct, and constant exchange of views lies at the core of Mark and Peter Anderson's joint authorship. They present their work as a fraternal collaboration beginning in childhood. In the book they speak both separately and together, and in dialogue with others, continuing a conversation in words and action that propels them through several decades of mutual support and challenge. Like the brothers Victor and Aladar Olgyay, who first built elegant international style buildings in Budapest, then put study of the potential for climate-responsive architecture on the map in the 1950s through their research at the Massachusetts Institute of Technology and Princeton University, they have developed a full body of work in which their respective voices are virtually indistinguishable—which ventures outside the bounds of conventional architecture. Like the Olgyays (who talked a lot about the sun and about science), they seek to understand how the evolving tools of present society can shape a more vigorous and purposeful future in building, carrying their explorations into the realm of the universities. Unlike the Olgyays, who invested their passion and intelligence in the publication of books like *Solar Control and Shading Devices* that could be used as standards by others, the Andersons present us with a more particularized, *ad hominem* experience, with an impressionistic map intended to prod (or is it plumb?) the imagination.

"A fundamental premise of our work is that art and its ambitions must play a much larger role in everyday life and in the definition of our culture and its physical construction." This, and similar expansive comments come in the Plumbing section of the book. "Plumbing," the Andersons explain, "is about ideas; what is carried in the pipes, what is carried by the building. . .plumbing is about space, sensuality, vegetables, density, and cities." The logic of this statement may seem obscure, but it is certainly the case that plumbing, or at least tubing, has become a dominant technique of our times. Plumbing, of the mundane, essential sort, has become so much a part of our fluent domestic arrangements that we forget to wonder at (or be concerned with the consequences of) the marvels of water springing from taps and of waste washing away into oblivion. Ducts and pipes, segregating flows of liquids and gases, make the engines of our cars work, and spread air and heat through our buildings. Segments of tube lift people up through buildings and ramp them into airplanes and thence across continents. Channels of highway slash through our cities and countryside creating hierarchies of access. We are aghast, yet no longer surprised, when skeins of plastic tubing and valves spring into action to nurture and sustain life in a hospital bed or when medical discussion turns to exploratory procedures that tunnel through arteries and the construction of bypasses. Tubular plumbing has become so ubiquitous that its metaphor permeates our ideas of health care, traffic engineering, mechanics, building construction, and yes, circulation.

Plumbing, (whose etymology is rooted, after all, in the use of lead) is robustly physical. It also connects, the Andersons remind us, to a larger networked infrastructure. To deal with the future, and the atmosphere of information in which it will materialize, we will also need to embrace less mechanical modes of thought; metaphors that are less separate; more inclusive and mysterious (like acupuncture); based on elements that are tinier, more pervasive (DNA), and more expansive; more generative, more energy-laden and diffuse; more filled with potential and surprise; vaporous...like various forms of cloud, perhaps.

DONLYN LYNDON

EARTHWORK. FRAMING. PLUMBING

FOR A LONG TIME WE HAVE BEEN AWARE OF THREE DISTINCT STRANDS IN OUR WORK. MORE RECENTLY, WE HAVE CLARIFIED OUR UNDERSTANDING OF THESE THREE STRANDS OF DESIGN AND CONSTRUCTION BY RELATING THEM TO THREE SEQUENTIAL PHASES IN BUILDING CONSTRUCTION: EARTHWORK, FRAMING, AND PLUMBING. ALL THREE TERMS ARE VERY SPECIFIC PHYSICAL ACTIONS IN THE SEQUENCE OF BUILDING. THEY ALSO COMPREHENSIVELY REPRESENT THE CONSTRUCTION PROCESS IN ITS THREE PRINCIPAL PHASES: PREPARING THE SITE AND FOUNDATIONS, ERECTING THE BUILDING, AND FINALLY CONNECTING IT INTO THE LARGER INFRASTRUCTURE. OUR INTEREST IN THESE TERMS RELATES BOTH TO THEIR MOST PRAGMATIC, EVERYDAY UNDERSTANDINGS AND TO A VARIETY OF ALTERNATE MEANINGS AND SPECULATIVE ASSOCIATIONS.

IT IS SIGNIFICANT THAT IN PRESENTING OUR WORK TOPICALLY IN THESE THREE STRANDS, RATHER THAN THROUGH A PROGRESSIVE SERIES OF PROJECTS, THE WORK NEVERTHELESS FALLS INTO A ROUGHLY CHRONOLOGICAL SEQUENCE OF IDEAS. THESE PHASES OF CONSTRUCTION MAY ALSO BE RECOGNIZED AS REPRESENTING PHASES OF PROGRESS—OR AT LEAST CHANGES OF FOCUS AND EXPANSIONS OF UNDERSTANDING, EXPERIENCE, AND BREADTH OF CONCERN—WITHIN OUR CAREERS AND BODY OF WORK.

AS BUILDING CONTRACTORS, WE KNOW THESE THREE TERMS AS DISTINCT PHASES OF CONSTRUCTION, EACH CONSTITUTING A MAJOR PUSH—DIVIDED BY TENSE DAYS OF PHONE CALLS, FAXES, HARANGUES, AND CAJOLING; PLOTTING OF SCHEDULES, MAKING 01043 OF LISTS; CHANGING SUITS FOR BOOTS, BULLDOZERS FOR HAMMERS, BOOM TRUCKS FOR SPRAY RIGS; MOBILIZING DIFFERENT CREWS AND COLLABORATORS: ENGINEERS, CONCRETE FINISHERS, PLUMBERS, WELDERS, CARPENTERS, CATERERS, AND MUSICIANS. AS ARCHITECTS, WE ARE THINKING OF THESE TERMS AS SHIFTING SCALES OF THOUGHT: SPECIFICALLY CONTEXT AND PARTICULARITY; RELATIONSHIP TO LARGER FRAMES OF REFERENCE, SYSTEMS, NETWORKS AND STRUCTURES OF THOUGHT; INVESTIGATIONS OF SPACE, EVENT, AND HUMAN EXPERIENCE.

AS A METAPHOR PARALLELING THE PRAGMATIC PHASES OF CONSTRUCTION, EARTHWORK 02200 REPRESENTS CLOSE ATTENTION TO THE PARTICULARITIES OF SITE AND CONTEXT. LIKE THE 02010 STUDIES OF ANY ISSUE, THERE ARE SIGNIFICANT LAYERS OF JOBSITE EARTH: VEGETAL TOPSOIL, MUD, SAND, CLAY, RUNNING GROUNDWATER, ROCK, LOOSE FILL, COMPACTED STRUCTURAL FILL, UNDISTURBED BEARING SOIL. BUILDING SOMETHING INVOLVES SMELLING AND READING THE EARTH, AND LEARNING FROM BULLDOZER OPERATORS AND OTHER EXPERTS WHO PRACTICE THE DEPTHS OF THEIR CRAFT EVERY DAY. EARTHWORK INVOLVES MAPPING THE TREE STEMS AND THEIR LIVING WEB OF ROOTS AMONGST THE FRAGILE AND IRREPLACEABLE NATIVE UNDERSTORY OF FERNS, MOSS, LICHENS, SALAL, AND HUCKLEBERRY. BUILDINGS ARE WOVEN INTO THIS DENSE SPACE OF ORGANIC MATTER. FIRST OF ALL THEY ARE WOVEN IN CONCEPTS, IN MAPS, AND ULTIMATELY THEY ARE PHYSICALLY WOVEN IN BY THE CAREFUL, MINUTE BY MINUTE PROCESSES OF DRAWING THE BUILDING UP FROM AND INTO ITS SITE. THE PROJECTS PRESENTED IN THE EARTHWORK SECTION OF THIS BOOK ARE MOST DIRECTLY CONCERNED WITH THE INVESTIGATION, UNDERSTANDING, AND DEVELOPMENT OF SPECIFIC IDEAS, CONTEXTUAL RELATIONSHIPS, DETAILS, AND METHODS OF CONSTRUCTION FOR SPECIFIC SITES.

WE FIRST BEGAN WORKING ON CONSTRUCTION PROJECTS WHEN WE WERE IN JUNIOR HIGH AND HIGH SCHOOL, BUILDING A SMALL VACATION CABIN WITH OUR PARENTS. THEN WE WORKED DIRECTLY FOR THE ARCHITECT OF THAT HOUSE ON VARIOUS PROJECTS OF HIS OWN. THROUGHOUT THE TIME THAT WE WERE IN COLLEGE AND GRADUATE SCHOOL—DURING WEEKENDS, SUMMERS, AND OCCASIONAL PERIODS OUT OF SCHOOL—WE BUILT DECKS, REMODELS, AND ADDITIONS FOR FRIENDS AND A BROADENING NETWORK OF REFERRALS. THIS IS THE BEGINNING OF WHAT MIGHT BE THOUGHT OF AS THE EARTHWORK PERIOD IN OUR CAREERS, WHEN WE FIRST WERE LEARNING TO BUILD, BUT REALLY THIS PERIOD EXTENDS MUCH FURTHER, TO THE TIME FOLLOWING GRADUATE SCHOOL, WHEN WE

PLUNGED INTO SERIOUS DEVELOPMENT OF OUR CONSTRUCTION COMPANY AND THE MAKING OF BUILDINGS. BAY PACIFIC CONSTRUCTION WAS
01060
FORMED AS AN OFFICIAL BUSINESS ENTERPRISE NEAR THE BEGINNING OF OUR GRADUATE STUDY AT THE HARVARD GRADUATE SCHOOL OF DESIGN. AFTER GRADUATION IT WAS THE CENTER OF OUR ACTIVITY FOR THE NEXT TEN YEARS.

THE FRAMING PERIOD IN OUR WORK, CONSIDERED CHRONOLOGICALLY, REPRESENTS PRIMARILY THE TIME IN THE DEVELOPMENT OF OUR CONSTRUCTION COMPANY WHEN, HAVING GOTTEN THE INITIAL COMPLEXITIES OF STARTING A BUSINESS UNDERWAY—LICENSES, CLIENTS, EMPLOYEES, EQUIPMENT, INTRODUCTIONS TO THE SCHOOL OF HARD KNOCKS—WE BEGAN TO STUDY AND UNDERSTAND THE SYSTEMS OF THINGS, RATHER THAN JUST THEIR PARTICULARITIES. THE FRAMING PERIOD DOES NOT SUPPLANT EARTHWORK; IT ADDS AN ADDITIONAL LAYER ON TOP OF IT, LIKE A BUILDING.

IN WOOD FRAME CONSTRUCTION, FRAMING, AS A VERB, REFERS TO THE NAILING TOGETHER AND ERECTION OF THE BUILDING'S STRUCTURAL FRAME. IN AMERICA AND IN MANY OTHER PARTS OF THE WORLD, FRAM-
06100
ING IS THE UNIQUELY ESSENTIAL SKILL OF HOUSE BUILDING. FRAMING, AS A NOUN, IS THE SKELETON SUPPORTING ALL THE CREATIVE AND PROGRAMMATIC FUNCTIONS OF THE HOUSE. AT SOME LEVEL, ALL OF OUR PROJECTS ARE AN INVESTIGATION OF STRUCTURE, MATERIALS, AND THE CRAFT OF ASSEMBLY. ALMOST ALL OF OUR WORK INVOLVES STRUCTURES THAT ARE A COMBINATION OF VARIOUS SYSTEMS: CONCRETE, STEEL, POST AND BEAM, TIMBERFRAME, WOOD PLATFORM FRAMING, BALLOON FRAMING, ENGINEERED WOOD TRUSS SYSTEMS, STRESS-SKIN SANDWICH PANELS, LIGHTWEIGHT CONCRETE PLANK. WE CALL THIS HYBRID FRAM-
06100
ING. WE WEAVE TOGETHER VARIOUS STRUCTURAL SYSTEMS—SOMETIMES TO LEARN SOMETHING NEW, TO ACCOMMODATE THE ENTHUSIASMS OF CLIENTS, TO WORK WITH INTERESTING SKILLS OF SUBCONTRACTORS AND EMPLOYEES, BUT MOST OF ALL TO HARNESS EACH SYSTEM'S UNIQUE CHARACTERISTICS TO ACHIEVE MOST EFFECTIVELY THE ARCHITECTURAL AMBITIONS OF THE PROJECT. THIS IS A VERY IMPORTANT POINT. WE LOVE EVERYTHING ABOUT THE PROCESS OF CONSTRUCTION, AND WE TRY VERY HARD TO DO A GOOD JOB WITH IT, BUT STRUCTURES AND MATERIALS AND CRAFT ARE NEVER THE DRIVING IDEA IN OUR WORK. CONSTRUCTION IS A RICH RESERVOIR OF IDEAS AND OPPORTUNITIES, AN ESSENTIAL MEDIUM OF ARCHITECTURAL INVESTIGATION, A STRICT DISCIPLINE, AND A TOOL; BUT ARCHITECTURE IS THE OBJECTIVE FOR US, NOT DESIGNING AND BUILDING.

HAVING SAID ALL OF THAT, THE FRAMING SECTION IS NOT REALLY ABOUT CONSTRUCTION FRAMING AT ALL, AT LEAST NOT IN THE BUILDING TRADE SENSE OF THE WORD. CONSTRUCTION FRAMING IS AN IMPORTANT ISSUE AT THE CENTER OF ALL OF THE PROJECTS IN THAT SECTION OF THIS BOOK, BUT IT IS NOT THE PRIMARY SUBJECT. BY THE ACCIDENTAL ACQUISITION
06100
OF FRAMING AS ONE OF OUR FEW AREAS OF HONEST TECHNICAL EXPERTISE, FRAMING AS A CONSTRUCTION TRADE HAS BECOME AN IMPORTANT MEDIUM WITHIN WHICH THE INVESTIGATION OF OUR BROADER DEFINITIONS OF FRAMING IS PLAYED OUT.

THE FRAMING SECTION RELATES OUR PROJECTS AND METHODS TO LARGER ORDERING SYSTEMS AND STRUCTURES OF THOUGHT. THIS INCLUDES PRAGMATIC EVERYDAY SYSTEMS—SUCH AS THE STANDARDIZED DIMENSIONS

MAKING THINGS

WE ALWAYS HAVE A HARD TIME SHOWING PEOPLE WHAT WE DO, BECAUSE WE REALLY DO A GREAT MANY DIFFERENT THINGS, WHICH WE THINK ARE ALL VERY TIGHTLY RELATED, BUT AMONG WHICH OTHER PEOPLE MIGHT NOT ALWAYS SEE THE CONNECTIONS. WE RARELY TALK ABOUT THE FULL RANGE OF PROJECTS WE ARE WORKING ON OR THINKING ABOUT, SO SOME PEOPLE END UP KNOWING US ONE WAY, AND SOME PEOPLE KNOW US ANOTHER, AND WE HAVE ALWAYS KIND OF ENJOYED THIS ANONYMITY OF SLIPPING IN AND OUT OF DIFFERENT WORLDS AT DIFFERENT TIMES, LETTING WHOMEVER WE ARE WORKING WITH AT THE TIME MAKE WHATEVER ASSUMPTIONS THEY WANT ABOUT WHO WE ARE AND WHAT WE ARE DOING. SOMETIMES THAT MEANS WORKING IN DIFFERENT PLACES, SOMETIMES WITHIN THE STRUCTURES OF DIFFERENT INDUSTRIES OR FIELDS, BEING CALLED DIFFERENT THINGS AND WORKING WITH DIFFERENT PEOPLE.

ONE CONSTANT, THOUGH, IS THE WAY WE WORK. WHETHER WE ARE BUILDING CONCRETE FORMS, WRITING ARTICLES, DESIGNING BUILDINGS, OR DREAMING UP NEW SCHEMES TO PURSUE, WE ALWAYS WORK TOGETHER. MARK AND I HAVE WORKED TOGETHER ON ALMOST EVERYTHING WE HAVE DONE OUR WHOLE LIVES. WHICH BRINGS ME TO THE OTHER CONSTANT, THAT WE ARE ALWAYS BUILDING AND MAKING THINGS, AND MORE RECENTLY SEEMINGLY NON-THINGS, WHICH ARE STILL REALLY THINGS WORKED UPON IN THING-LIKE WAYS.

WE HAVE ALWAYS THOUGHT OF "MAKING" AS A MUCH MORE DESCRIPTIVE TERM FOR WHAT WE DO THAN EITHER DESIGNING OR BUILDING. WHEN PEOPLE DO HEAR THAT WE ARE BOTH ARCHITECTS AND BUILDERS, THEY SOMETIMES IMAGINE THAT WE ARE PART OF THAT NEBULOUS WORLD OF "DESIGN-BUILD," WHICH WE ARE NOT OPPOSED TO IN CONCEPT, BUT WHICH SEEMS SO OFTEN TO INVOLVE RESULTS THAT ARE NOT PARTICULARLY GOOD EXAMPLES OF EITHER DESIGNING OR

AND CONNECTION DETAILS COMMON TO NORTH AMERICAN LIGHT FRAME CONSTRUCTION; THE STANDARDIZED FILING INDEX OF THE CONSTRUCTION SPECIFICATION INSTITUTE (CSI); THE POTENTIAL TO MAKE BUILDINGS MORE AFFORDABLE, MORE FLEXIBLE, MORE CREATIVE AND MORE HUMANE BY SYSTEMATIZING SIGNIFICANT ELEMENTS OF CONSTRUCTION DELIVERY AND ADMINISTRATION. IT ALSO INCLUDES LARGER CONSTRUCTED SYSTEMS OF ASSUMPTIONS AND PRACTICE, LIKE GLOBALIZATION AND FREE TRADE.

BUILDING. SCULPTORS AND PAINTERS "MAKE" ART; ONE RARELY HEARS THE TERM "DESIGNING" OR "BUILDING" IN RELATION TO THOSE CREATIVE DISCIPLINES. WHEN MARK AND I WERE LITTLE, WE WOULD "MAKE" TREE HOUSES AND LEGO BLOCK CITIES AND TINKERTOY CONTRAPTIONS. MARK USED TO DIG AIRPLANES. WHEN HE WANTED TO PLAY IN AN AIRPLANE, HE DIDN'T HAVE THE TIME OR RESOURCES OR PATIENCE TO PLAN OUT AND MANUFACTURE A WOOD AND FABRIC VERSION. HE JUST GOT A SHOVEL AND DUG OUT THE SHAPE OF A PLANE IN THE BACK YARD, SAT DOWN AND STARTED MAKING MOTOR NOISES. NOISES, ALSO, ARE A GOOD EXAMPLE HERE. YOU DON'T DESIGN NOISES AND THEN BUILD THEM. IF YOU WANT A NOISE, YOU MAKE IT. IF YOU DON'T LIKE IT, YOU KEEP MAKING NOISES UNTIL YOU FIND ONE YOU LIKE. THAT IS MAYBE A BETTER DESCRIPTION OF THE WAY WE DO THINGS THAN ANYTHING ELSE IS.

WHEN PEOPLE HEAR US TALK ABOUT MAKING THINGS, THE IMMEDIATE IMAGES ARE OF BUILDINGS—MOSTLY THE WOOD BUILDINGS PEOPLE KNOW US FOR. BUT THERE ARE MANY OTHER THINGS WE ARE ALWAYS MAKING THAT MIGHT BE LESS OBVIOUS. SOME ARE CLOSELY RELATED TO NARROWER DEFINITIONS OF THE FIELD OF ARCHITECTURE, LIKE ENTERING COMPETITIONS OR OCCASIONALLY WRITING SOMETHING OR TEACHING. SOMETIMES IT IS A COLLABORATIVE PROJECT WITH PEOPLE IN OTHER FIELDS, LIKE WORKING WITH CHOREOGRAPHERS AND SOUND ARTISTS. OFTEN THE THINGS WE ARE BUILDING ARE NOT PHYSICAL STRUCTURES, BUT MECHANISMS FOR ACCOMPLISHING OTHER THINGS, AS IN ESTABLISHING BUSINESS VENTURES AND IDENTITIES, SETTING UP NON-PROFIT STRUCTURES FOR ACHIEVING SOME PURPOSE, ORGANIZING CONFERENCES, OR PUTTING TOGETHER RESEARCH TRIPS OR STUDY TOURS WITH STUDENTS.

BASICALLY, THE FRAMING SECTION IS ABOUT CONSTRUCTION SYSTEMS AND STANDARDS, PREFABRICATION AND INDUSTRY RATIONALIZATION, ENTREPRENEURSHIP AND EVERYDAY BUSINESS PRACTICE, INTERNATIONAL TRADE AND MACRO-ECONOMICS, AND THE STRUCTURAL RELATIONSHIPS AMONG ARCHITECTURE, SOCIAL POLICY, AND QUALITY OF LIFE. DON'T BE FOOLED BY ALL OF THE PICTURES OF 2X4S.

CHRONOLOGICALLY, THE FRAMING SECTION COINCIDES WITH THE PERIOD IN OUR CONSTRUCTION COMPANY WHEN WE HAD A RELATIVELY LARGE NUMBER OF EMPLOYEES. AT THAT TIME, WE WERE CONCERNED WITH ESTABLISHING RATIONALIZED SYSTEMS FOR ALL TYPES OF OPERATIONS WITHIN OUR COMPANY. WE WERE BUILDING LARGER AND MORE COMPLEX WORK AND WERE THEREFORE INVOLVED IN LEARNING MANY NEW SYSTEMS AND THEIR INTERRELATIONSHIPS. ADDITIONALLY, THIS WAS A TIME WHEN WE WERE DOING A LOT OF BUILDING, DESIGNING, AND TEACHING IN JAPAN, WHICH—LIKE LEARNING A NEW LANGUAGE—FORCED US TO BEGIN THINKING VERY SYSTEMATICALLY ABOUT OUR METHODS AND MATERIALS OF CONSTRUCTION. IN MANY WAYS, JAPAN HAS BEEN FOR US A SCHOOL, A LABORATORY, A TOOL, AND A MIRROR, TEACHING US THINGS WE NEVER KNEW ABOUT THE WORLD AND OUR WORK.

THE IDEA OF PLUMBING, AS WE CONSIDER IT HERE, CANNOT BE STRICTLY RELATED TO A CERTAIN MOMENT IN OUR WORK. IN THE BUILDING TRADE, ESSENTIALLY ALL OF OUR WORKS—FROM HOUSES TO DRAWINGS TO GALLERY INSTALLATIONS, CONTAIN PLAIN, ORDINARY, FUNCTIONING PIPES, HOSES, AND WIRES, WHICH IN TURN CHANNEL WATER, GAS, AND ELECTRICITY—ALL OR SOME OF THE BASIC UTILITIES THAT MAY REASONABLY BE FILED UNDER THE HEADING OF PLUMBING. WE HAVE NEVER BEEN PROFESSIONAL PLUMBERS. PLUMBING AS A BUILDING OR BUSINESS ACTIVITY HAS NEVER CAPTURED OUR IMAGINATION IN THE SAME WAY THAT WORKING WITH EARTH, OR WOOD, OR ALMOST ANYTHING ELSE HAS. BUT SOMEHOW WE HAVE ALWAYS BEEN UP TO OUR ELBOWS IN SOME PLUMBING PROJECT OR ANOTHER. ONE OF OUR EARLIEST CONSTRUCTION CONTRACTS INVOLVED A GREAT DEAL OF UNDERGROUND PLUMBING: INSTALLING WATER PIPES AND FIRE-HYDRANT SYSTEMS. WE HAD THIS JOB AT A TIME WHEN WE WERE DOING ALL OF THE LABOR OURSELVES. THE UNDERGROUND WORK WAS GREAT—MUD, LARGE-DIAMETER PIPES, FOUL-SMELLING GREASE, RUBBER GASKETS, BACKHOES AND BULLDOZERS, BEAUTIFUL CAST-IRON PUMPS AND HYDRANTS, INTRICATE BRONZE VALVES AND MANIFOLDS. AMAZING.

THE FIRE HYDRANTS LEAKED AND HAD TO BE DUG UP. THE GASKETS WERE IN BACKWARDS. WE LEFT TOWN. PETER LEFT FOR ITALY TO WORK AS A CARPENTER ON A SMALL FARM IN TUSCANY. I WENT TO GERMANY AND WORKED WITH TURKS, SERBS, AND CALABRIANS POURING CONCRETE IN MUNICH. THIS FIRST OF SEVERAL PLUMBING FIASCOS SHOULD HAVE BEEN

A WARNING—STICK TO YOUR KNITTING, LEARN ONE TRADE AND DO IT WELL. WE'VE NEVER TAKEN, OR BEEN OFFERED, ANOTHER FIRE HYDRANT CONTRACT. ON THE OTHER HAND, WE'VE AVOIDED EXTRAPOLATING THE LESSONS OF THAT MISADVENTURE INTO ANY MORE BROADLY LIMITING CONCLUSIONS.

THE TERM PLUMBING, FOR THE PURPOSES OF THE PROJECTS PRESENTED IN THAT SECTION, INCLUDES THE FUNCTIONAL ISSUES OF REGULAR PIPES. BEYOND THAT, PLUMBING IS ABOUT IDEAS: WHAT IS CARRIED IN THE PIPES, WHAT IS CARRIED BY THE BUILDING. PLUMBING THE DEPTHS, LOOKING FOR ANSWERS. THESE ARE NOT THE PRIMARY METAPHORS WE WISH TO EMPHASIZE. PLUMBING FOR OUR PURPOSES IS ABOUT SPACE AND HUMAN EXPERIENCE. IN THE SERIES OF PROJECTS PRESENTED IN THAT SECTION, PLUMBING IS ABOUT SPACE, SENSUALITY, VEGETABLES, DENSITY, AND CITIES.

AS PLUMBING ALWAYS INVOLVES SYSTEMS AND CONNECTIONS AND NETWORKS, THIS CATEGORY OVERLAPS SOMEWHAT WITH OUR DEFINITIONS OF FRAMING. IN FRAMING, HOWEVER, THE SYSTEMS ARE NOT MATERIAL THEMSELVES; THEY ARE ONLY CONCEPTUAL STRUCTURES THAT PEOPLE USE TO DEFINE MATERIAL RELATIONSHIPS BETWEEN CLEARLY IDENTIFIABLE THINGS. PLUMBING IS VERY DIFFERENT. PLUMBING SYSTEMS ARE 100 PERCENT REAL ₁₅₄₀₀ MATERIAL AND AT THE SAME TIME VERY ABSTRACT. THE NETWORK (SHEET METAL, PIPE, WIRE, HOSE) IS REAL, THE STUFF THAT IT CARRIES (AIR, WATER, ELECTRICITY, GAS) IS REAL, AND THE EFFECT THAT IS CARRIED (WARMTH, COOLNESS, HUMIDITY, LIGHT, PRESSURE, PULSE, MOTION, DIRECTION, PATTERN, SEQUENCE, FLOW) IS ALSO REAL. IT IS ALL SO BACKGROUND, SO MINIMAL AND ABSTRACT. ONLY THE EFFECT REALLY MATTERS. THE EFFECT IS THE ARCHITECTURE, NOT THE PIPES AND THEIR CONTENTS.

SOME OF THIS STARTED OUT IN OUR THINKING ABOUT NEW NETWORKS AND SYSTEMS—LIKE THE INTERNET—WHICH ARE PHYSICAL IN ONE SENSE, BUT ARE PRIMARILY IMPORTANT AND EXCITING TO EVERYONE BECAUSE THEY ARE EFFECTIVELY VIRTUAL. WE ARE VERY INTERESTED IN THESE THINGS: COMPUTERS, VIRTUAL SPACE, E-COMMERCE. WE EVEN HAVE A WEBSITE WITH A SHOPPING CART SYSTEM, ALTHOUGH WE HAVE NOT YET FIGURED OUT WHAT WE'RE SELLING. ON THE OTHER HAND, WE LIKE THINGS TO BE PHYSICAL. WE LIKE TO MAKE THINGS. BEYOND THAT, WE STRUGGLE WITH THE POLITICAL IMPLICATIONS OF IDEAS THAT ARE DISCONNECTED FROM MATERIAL REALITY. IN TERMS OF PLUMBING, WE CAN BEGIN TO UNDERSTAND AND EXPERIENCE SPACE—EVEN BEGIN TO CARVE, DEFINE, AND CREATE SPACE—IN WAYS THAT ARE ABSTRACT, FACILITATED BY THE TECHNOLOGIES OF ELECTRONIC EVENTS, YET FULLY AND EMPHATICALLY REAL. PLUMBING ONLY LOOKS ABSTRACT; ITS PHYSICAL IMPACT IN SPACE IS NOT CONCEPTUAL AT ALL. PIPES, WIRES, HOSES, BLADDERS, MUD, TIME, SPACE, EVENT, ARCHITECTURE—THAT IS WHAT THE PLUMBING SECTION IS ALL ABOUT.

JUST AS A COMPLETED BUILDING IS CONSTRUCTED THROUGH PHASES OF THOUGHT AND INTENSE ACTIVITY, AS SUB-ASSEMBLIES ARE SIMULTANEOUSLY WOVEN TOGETHER INTO ONE INTERRELATED WHOLE, WE THINK EACH STRAND IN OUR WORK IS CLEARLY PRESENT ₁₃₀₂₀ AND WOVEN INTO EACH OF OUR PROJECTS. THIS IS TRUE WHETHER IT IS THE CONSTRUCTION OF A HOUSE, THE IMAGINING OF A NEW PREFABRICATION SYSTEM, THE FORMATION OF A NEW BUSINESS, OR THE MAKING OF A PUBLIC ART INSTALLATION. AS HARD AS WE HAVE TRIED TO PRESENT OUR PROJECTS IN RELATIONSHIP TO THE EXTENDED MEANINGS OF DIVISION INTO SECTIONS ON EARTHWORK, FRAMING, AND PLUMBING, ULTIMATELY WE WOULD LIKE ALL OF OUR PROJECTS TO BE UNDERSTOOD AS SERIOUS THOUGHTS ABOUT THE RELATIONSHIP OF THESE IDEAS CONSIDERED TOGETHER.

02200

EARTHWORK

VIEW FROM PRAIRIE LADDER SkyBarge LOOKING DOWN INTO EarthPlane, EARLY SPRING.

1 LANDSCAPES

OUR UNDERSTANDING OF THE RELATIONSHIP BETWEEN BUILT STRUCTURES AND THEIR CONTEXTS HAS GROWN INCREMENTALLY, PROGRESSING FROM SIMPLE INTUITION AND PRACTICAL NECESSITY IN EARLY PROJECTS THROUGH INCREASINGLY CONSCIOUS STUDY AND STRUCTURED INTENTION WITH EACH NEW EXPERIENCE. WHILE ANY OF THE PROJECTS CAN SERVE AS A STARTING POINT, WE HAVE FOUND IT MOST CLEAR TO BEGIN WITH THE PRAIRIE LADDER PROJECT IN WHICH THE PROGRAM IDENTIFIED AND ANALYZED THE FACTORS AFFECTING THE PLACEMENT OF BUILT STRUCTURES IN AN ENVIRONMENT. STRIPPED OF THE SPECIFIC PROGRAMMATIC REQUIREMENTS ASSOCIATED WITH SHELTER OR CITIES, THIS SERIES OF STRUCTURES ON THE TEXAS PRAIRIE FORCED AND FACILITATED A CLARIFICATION IN ALL OUR WORK CONCERNING HOW WE APPROACH THE SPACES AND PLACES INTO WHICH WE INTRODUCE NEW ELEMENTS.

HORIZON VIEW THROUGH PRAIRIE LADDER SKYBARGE.

PERHAPS WORKING WITH THE LANDSCAPE OF OPEN PRAIRIE HAS SO CLEARLY AFFECTED OUR UNDERSTANDING OF SPACE BECAUSE IT IS SO DIFFERENT FROM THE PLACES WE HAVE KNOWN BETTER. WE GREW UP IN THE PACIFIC NORTHWEST, IN A LANDSCAPE OF MOUNTAINS AND TREES, SHORELINES, LOW FOGS AND MISTS — SPACE WITHIN SPACE WITHIN HUMAN-ACCESSIBLE SPACE. IF WE WANTED TO CLIMB INTO THE SKY WE COULD RUN UP A HILL OR CLIMB A HUGE TREE OR JUST JUMP UP SIX INCHES INTO A CLOUD. IF WE WANTED TO SINK DOWN INTO THE WARM, WELCOMING EARTH, WE COULD SLIP DOWN A SLUG-SLIMY CREEK BANK OR JUST WIGGLE OUR FEET SLOWLY DEEPER AND DEEPER INTO A MUD PUDDLE OR A WET SAND BEACH. IN A PLACE LIKE THE NORTHWEST, ALL THE EARTH AND THE SKY FLOW TOGETHER INTO ONE SEAMLESSLY INHABITABLE SPACE. SOMETIMES IT IS CLAUSTROPHOBIC AND OVERWHELMING. THEN WE HEAD SOUTH AND EAST, OVER THE MOUNTAINS AND INTO THE DESERTS, ACROSS THE PALOUSE TO THE GREAT PLAINS, INTO THE HARD-LINE OPENNESS OF THE MIDDLE OF AMERICA. SOMETIMES WHEN WE'RE DRIVING OUT INTO THE OPEN, OR PEERING THROUGH FLAPPING WIPERS INTO UNFOLDING DENSITIES OF FOG, IT SEEMS LIKE WE ARE APPROACHING SOME COMPREHENSION OF WHAT SPACE MEANS TO HUMAN BEINGS AND THEIR AMBITIONS, AND BIG UNDERSTANDINGS.

The Prairie Ladder project began as a commission from the Connemara Conservancy, an organization with large land holdings in central Texas, with the stated purpose of preserving, protecting, and honoring the prairie landscape. Each year a few artists are selected and given funding to produce an installation on the land, which supports and brings attention to the foundation's mission. Working together with our friend and frequent collaborator Cameron Schoepp, a sculptor from Fort Worth, Texas, we spent a great deal of time on the site, synthesizing our own experience of this place with the larger tradition of human settlement on the archetypal landscape of the western prairie.

As the project developed, we envisioned a series of big, ladder-related objects spread out all over a large swath of Texas, each focusing on a singular, pure experience of the prairie as a trinity of horizon, earth, and sky. We became intensely interested in this fundamentally American landscape in which human beings have no particular place, where physical and conceptual space can only be understood as a line between the sky, which is no home for human beings, and the belowground, which is no home for human beings.

The selection of the ladder as an element common to each of the works introduces a vertical axis, marking a departure from the natural horizontal axis of the prairie. The ladder also provides a human scale, and proclaims human defiance of the horizontal limitations of the earth. This real or implied activity of vertical movement on the prairie, whether up into the sky or down into the earth, is the defining characteristic of placemaking—of human settlement or intervention in the existing primal environment.

SUNCELLAR

EARTHPLANE/SKYBARGE

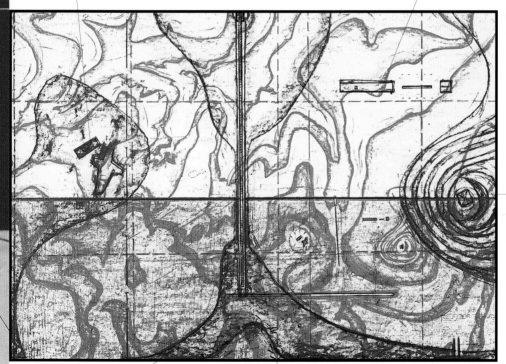

DALLAS, TEXAS 1989-1994
WITH CAMERON SCHOEPP

WEATHERSTATION

TERMINUS

SITE PLAN AT TWO SCALES FROM SUITE OF SIX
PRAIRIE LADDER LITHOGRAPHS PRODUCED FROM
CHARCOAL RUBBINGS OF CONCRETE AND STEEL
MODELS, 1994. COLLECTION SAN FRANCISCO
MUSEUM OF MODERN ART.

WATERBRIDGE

In **EarthPlane/SkyBarge**, we dug down into the earth and built up into the sky and thought about the human ambition to penetrate and possess the earth and the sky and always to stare at and aspire towards the distant line in between. The transparent SkyBarge points into the wind and provides for the climber an oculus focused on the horizon from whence the winds of memory and aspiration blow. EarthPlane cuts open the freshness of the earth and places the inhabitant at eye level with the ground plane. Buried, the viewer is one with the horizon. These vehicles of imagined flight are arrested by the emphatic ladder, which interrupts their flowing motion across the placeless prairie. As always, we had a lot of fun with backhoes and cranes and steel and cable and fiberglass and perforated aluminum and lots of people scratching their heads and wondering what on earth we were doing as they cheerfully pitched in with hard work and all the experience and wisdom of their trades. **WeatherStation** provides a pure and minimal focus on the rotation of the changing/changeless sky. Existing as an object when approached from the exterior, once entered, it becomes an instrument of observation, providing a vantage point and false horizon to facilitate the understanding of the sky as a separate element, without its earthbound delimitations. **SunCellar** empties a vast cube of earth cut to just below the level of the groundwater. Human access is provided by a heavy lidded ramp and a ladder suspended by cable in a bottomless well. Angled lenses focus sunlight into the depths of the cube to reflect from the floor of water onto the steel-restrained earthen walls and ceiling. The inhabitant stands suspended on a catwalk in the center of this storehouse of aqueous, rippling light, blinded, following a dark descent away from the sky. **Terminus** provides a rail-thin line across the prairie, turning upward to form a ladder cabled into the sky. Terminus refers to infinite passage across the prairie and to the nameless, placeless endpoint imagined only as a terminus to travel rather than as a place of arrival: the mythic railroad serving as a metaphor for life on the prairie. **WaterBridge** brings the subterranean aquifer to the waterless surface of the prairie in the form of a horizontal bridge of suspended water. The span traverses at horizon level the full length of a narrow incision in the earth, with steel plate walls cutting down to the water table and the life blood of the prairie.

OPPOSITE PAGE: PRAIRIE LADDER SITE MODEL.
FLAME CUT STEEL. THIS PAGE: SKYBARGE UNDER
CONSTRUCTION. INSET: WEATHERSTATION
MODEL. STEEL, CONCRETE, AND CAST RESIN.

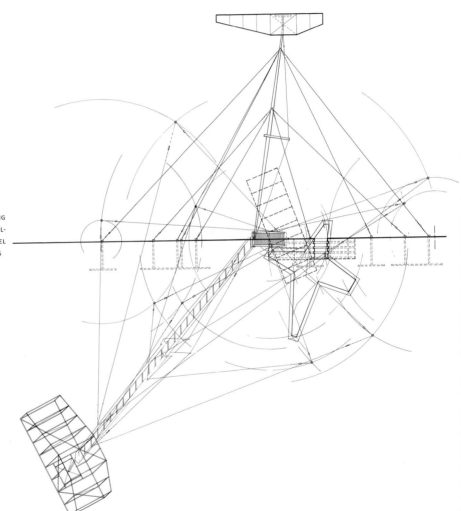

THIS PAGE: SECTION/PLAN/AXONOMETRIC DRAWING OF EarthPlane/SkyBarge ON HORIZON LINE. FOL-LOWING PAGES: DETAIL OF TERMINUS MODEL. STEEL AND CONCRETE. RIGHT: *FLASH PONTIAC*. CROSSING SASKATCHEWAN, 1988.

2 STEEP HILLS AND WATERFRONT

SITTING ON A HIGH BANK OF HARSTINE ISLAND IN SOUTH PUGET SOUND, THE JOHNSON VACATION HOUSE IS CONCEIVED AS A FORT: A FORT ON A RAFT IN A FOREST. THE INTERIOR AND EXTERIOR LIVING SPACES ARE CONSTRUCTED AS PLATFORMS OF WOOD, ALLOWING THE NATURAL VEGETATION TO FILL UP TO THE HOUSE ON ALL SIDES WITHOUT DISTURBANCE. IT IS MEANT TO BE FUN AND ADVENTURE-FILLED, A RETREAT WITH MULTIPLE STAIRS AND PASSAGES, SURPRISING LOOKOUTS, MYSTERIOUS BALCONIES, A SLEEPING TOWER AIMED AT THE MOON. THE SITE IS SMALL AND SUR- ROUNDED BY OTHER CABINS, BUT THE NARROW ENTRY TUNNEL IN THE CENTER OF THE BLUNT, PROTECTIVE FACADE PASSES THROUGH THE BUILDING AND OPENS ON A PRIVATE COURT SURROUNDED ONLY BY BALCONIES, TOWERS, AND TREES. THE VIEWS FROM WITHIN THIS RAFT-LIKE ENCAMPMENT ARE CAREFULLY DIRECTED TO THE FOREST, PUGET SOUND, AND THE OLYMPIC MOUNTAINS. EVEN THE FURTHEST BACK ROOMS ON THE STREET SIDE PEER AROUND THE INTERVENING CONSTRUCTIONS, ALLOWING ALL SPACES TO SEE THE WATER AND SHARE IN THE LIGHT FROM THE NARROWEST WESTERN END OF THE SITE.

BECAUSE OF THE SITE'S REMOTE LOCATION, WE MINIMIZED THE NEED FOR MULTIPLE SUBCONTRACTORS BY THE CHOICE OF MATERIALS AND THE OVERALL PLANS. WE DESIGNED THE DETAILS AND THE STAGING OF THE CONSTRUCTION TO ALLOW OUR OWN CARPENTRY CREW TO PROVIDE ALMOST ALL THE REQUIRED CRAFT SKILLS FROM FRAMING THROUGH FINISH. THE ENTIRE HOUSE, INSIDE AND OUT, IS BUILT WITH CONSTRUCTION-GRADE LUMBER AND FRAMING-STYLE FINISH CARPENTRY.

JOHNSON VACATION HOUSE,
HARSTINE ISLAND, WASHINGTON 1990.

GETTING STARTED

During and between the periods we were in high school, college, and graduate school, we spent a lot of time building things. Sometimes we were working for architects, but most often we were designing these increasingly complex projects ourselves. We worked out a lot of the building issues in rough models, followed by simple drawings just sufficient to cover the basics of dimensions and materials-ordering needs. Rarely did these designs have to be communicated to anyone other than us. Our improbably credulous clients relied, we believe, more on our earnestness than on a clear understanding of what we were proposing to do.

One project led to another, the opportunity usually based on the need to solve some particular problem, most often having some direct relationship to rotting wood or leaking roofs caused by previous building errors. Fixing other people's mistakes is an amazingly effective education. Much of what we know now about flashings, sealants, and proper ventilation techniques we learned by pulling handfuls of soggy, decomposed structural members out of walls and attics and figuring out how to rebuild a solid new base, in a way that would never leak or rot again.

Interesting as these experiences in building pathology were, our greater ambitions were to do our own projects from the ground up. This shift was not easy; it's hard to get the chance to do something unless you have already proven you can do it. Clients were hard to find, so we decided to approach some banks about financing a speculative project. After many polite refusals—citing our minimal experience and non-existent assets—we tried the new tactic of asking for even more money so that we could do multiple projects at once. We pitched the scheme to an aggressive cowboy banker who said he trusted us, and we were off and running in the new-home construction business.

We soon learned that fixing other people's problems as a starting point for opportunity was not restricted to the remodeling business. We began to specialize in taking on property with steep slopes or other difficult site conditions that made land cheap to buy but difficult to develop. Our first two homes were on adjacent hillside sites that a developer had been trying to sell for years with no success. We worked carefully with the steep slopes, stepping the interior spaces and simple shed rooflines with the topography, which reduced foundation costs and made for more interesting open spaces.

Those two houses were very important to us for establishing future work and for learning how to go about changing directions when we wanted to or needed to. The Tacoma newspaper ran a story about them on the front page of the business section, with a big color picture of us and the headline, "Going Up a Hill to Keep Costs Down," making a big issue of how inexpensively we could build homes on difficult sites. Of course they left out the part about how we barely broke even on the projects, and didn't pay ourselves for design or labor, but it worked to get several subsequent projects with interesting sites (and unreasonably low expectations of building costs). For many years we had a Yellow Pages ad in the local directories that said "New Construction—Steep Hills and Waterfront." We never thought the ads themselves brought in any projects, but the declaration of our specialization proved to be a self-fulfilling prophecy.

The next several years we had the chance to design and build many houses, working with the same general concept of light-seeking roofs and multi-level floorplans woven into the trees and slopes of difficult sites. With each project we tried new things, got new ideas, and learned new ways to work with the land, the details, and the materials. There were no sudden shifts in our work, as each new project built directly on the last.

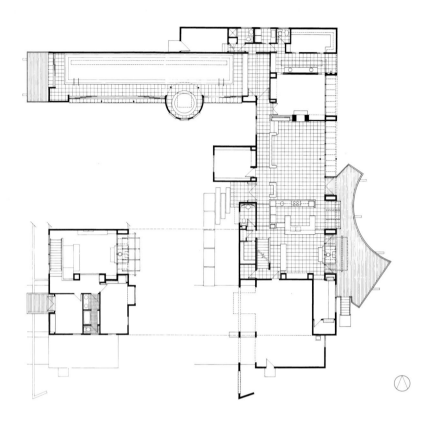

ELL RESIDENCE,
SEATTLE, WASHINGTON 1994.

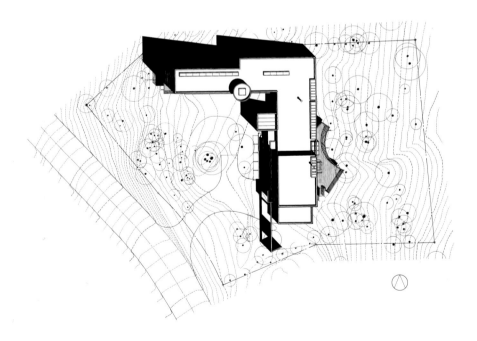

DIGGING

There are textbooks about proper and efficient excavation practice. [01091] They are all wrong, even—often enough—when viewed from a strictly economic standpoint. This has to do with what we think of as the problem of gross rationality, as opposed to fine-grained rationality, which takes into account the true complexities, interdependencies, and infinite rippling consequences of real events in the real world. Peter and I have a knee-jerk distaste for simplistic reasoning, gross rationality, or smug, self-certain decision-making. It's very hard for us to make decisions, to choose, to plan ahead. There are too many variables, too many outstanding opportunities, too many doubts. Still, we get a lot of stuff done, because we can't stay away from the world of commerce and machines. [00240] Money has its own fine-grained, dynamic logic. So do machines. Bulldozers cost $100 an hour, and can cost ten times that amount in semi-repairable damage if they make a mistake.

DIRT AND MACHINES

THIS IS THE WAY IT WORKS ON A JOB SITE IN THE TREES. ITS RAINING, ITS FOGGY, AND THE UNDER-BRUSH IS TOO THICK TO WALK THROUGH. MAC FIELDS DRIVES UP WITH HIS DUMP TRUCKS, LOADER, AND SIX-WAY BLADE. HIS SON PHIL UNSHACKLES THE EQUIPMENT AND DRIVES IT DOWN OFF THEIR TRAILERS WHILE MAC AND I STARE INTO THE TREES AND BRUSH, TALKING THROUGH THE PLAN OF ATTACK. DURING THE DESIGN PROCESS, PETER AND I HAVE FOUGHT THROUGH THE UNDER-BRUSH MANY TIMES, MEASURING, MAPPING, [00230] THINKING, AND REELING OUT FLUORESCENT ORANGE [01050] MARKER TAPE TO SECTION OFF THE PERIMETERS OF FELLING AND SCRAPING AND DIGGING.

IT ALWAYS SEEMS ON CLEARING AND EXCAVATION DAYS LIKE WE'RE FIGHTING A BATTLE. THERE ARE STRATEGIES, TACTICS, ACCIDENTS, AND SURPRISES, OFTEN EVEN SOME HIGH-LEVEL SHUTTLE DIPLOMACY [01043] **GOING ON SOMEWHERE WITH THE NEIGHBORS. ITS MUDDY, ITS PAINFUL AND EXHAUSTING, SOMETIMES A LITTLE DANGEROUS, DEFINITELY NOISY AND CON-FUSING, AND ITS RANK WITH THE SMELL OF FRESH-LY CUT EARTH AND DIESEL FUMES. AND FOR THAT MATTER WE'RE DESTROYING LIFE.** [02070] **PUSHING THROUGH THE BLACKBERRIES AND CEDARS, CROSS-ING THE WATERCOURSES, STEPPING ON SLUGS, AND DIGGING INTO THE STEAMING, VEGETABLE EARTH, YOU CAN'T HELP BUT THINK ABOUT THAT.**

Clearing and excavating is complicated for many reasons, partly because this beginning step in the construction process sets the [02100] stage for so many operations on the site thereafter. For example, you need space for the building itself, plus you need space to stack [01043] materials, to access cranes, forklifts, and backhoes to all sides of the building. You need a flat site adequate to stage a concrete pump truck, and parking for dozens of workers. The textbook solution is to clear a large perimeter and construct a roadway base around the foundation from which to stage the construction. Although this is highly rational from an efficient engineering point of view, there are many problems with this approach. Sites can be [02900] landscaped (who ever took this word away from the painters, recast it as a verb, and handed it over to the design and construction industry as a decorating activity at the end of the building process?), but it is essentially impossible to replant the diverse native understory of Northwest forests. Trees themselves are easier to replace, although rarely at the size, maturity, and diversity of what has been removed. There is an increasing recognition of the [02900] ecological importance of preserving diverse natural landscapes, and we believe that this can be accomplished even on individual house sites. We don't like hybrid rhododendrons; we like the look and feel and smell of the Northwest forest.

There are broader issues of environmental economic efficiency in [00240] minimizing the excavation impact as well. The less dirt that needs to be moved in or out, the less general consumption of earth, gravel, plants, fuel, and re-landscaping energy, the less generation of waste, and the less expenditure of time and money. Our projects often run on very tight budgets, with little money allocated to landscape design and construction. For millions of reasons, both lofty and pragmatic, we go to great lengths to tuck our buildings into the land with minimal disturbance to the existing nature of the site. Saving the ground involves more than writing a note on the site plan—you have to be there, which is also more fun.

TREES AND SMOKE

Dropping trees is trickier than one might think. You can cut them, or you can push them over with the dozer. Pushing them over is fastest and cleanest and safest because you have more control over the speed and direction of the drop, and, best of all, the roots are levered out cleanly by the weight of the falling tree. This process is straightforward for small- to medium-sized trees within the center of the excavation. The problems come with trees too big for the dozer to push, or trees at the edge of the foundation hole. When a tree is pushed, the roots tear up a large ball of earth as broad as the canopy of the tree, ripping out all the understory vegetation and topsoil along with it. Inside the cut, this is perfect—you need to get all the roots and organic matter out of the foundation area.

02070

Since we are trying to save all the trees and groundcover within a few feet of the foundation, any trees near the perimeter of the foundation area, whether inside or out, need to be cut with a chainsaw and felled in a manner that does the least damage possible. This means dropping the trees into the area that will be excavated, rather than outward into the brush, which would require dragging the tree out and leaving a trail of damage. Even the trees that are pushed over are carefully directed into the center rather than outward. This means that the trees are often pulled rather than pushed, to avoid driving the bulldozer outside the perimeter to the back of the tree. Sometimes we can pull it with a chain, or a cable and winch, depending on the machines available. If we decide to pull with a cable, I step into the bucket of the machine and am lifted as high as possible to attach a shackle around the tree at the point of maximum leverage. Often Mac just catches the tree with the back of the blade and pulls it slowly down on top of his roll cage. After climbing out from under, I and Mac cut the bulldozer out from under the tree with chainsaws.

Frequently Mac will jump down from his machine and take over the saw. He can tell which trees have internal stresses and twists, and he always takes those down himself. Alders and Madronas are the most dangerous. Cedars and fir are more predictable. I run along all the dropped trees sawing off the boughs and dragging them to the fire. Mac has a very specific method for stacking fires, and I follow it carefully. Clearing fires are a major air pollution problem. Really, everything should be hauled off and recycled, something which has only recently become much of a possibility. Stumps, full of rocks and dirt in their tangled roots, can not be sawn or chipped and can only be burned or brought to a landfill. A single stump root is often a full dump truck load. There are lots of problems with this process no matter which system is used. The best course is to minimize taking trees in the first place. But the fires with their broad envelopes
15550
of heat and the machines clanking in and out of view through the
15525
smoke and fog are a fantastic experience.

I POINT OUT MY STRATEGY TO MAC. HE LISTENS TO THE BIG IDEA, WHAT IS TO BE SAVED, WHAT IS TO BE CUT, BUT MAC IS IN CHARGE OF THE TACTICS. THIS MAKES MY JOB MORE DIFFICULT IN THAT I'M DIRECTING THE BIG PICTURE WHILE REACTING TO THE DYNAMIC AND FREQUENTLY UNEXPECTED FLOW OF THE MACHINES. IT HAS TO BE DYNAMIC, SINCE SEVERAL MINDS ARE AT WORK ON A CONSTANTLY SHIFTING PROBLEM. THIS IS ONE REASON WE ARE ALWAYS REASSESSING THE TYPICAL, TOP-DOWN HIERARCHY OF THE CONSTRUCTION PROCESS AND TRADITIONAL FORMATS FOR WORKING
01043
DRAWINGS AND SPECIFICATIONS. THE ENGAGED MIND OF AN EXPERIENCED CONSTRUCTION WORKER IS ESSENTIAL TO GOOD DESIGN AND BUILDING.

THE CLEARING PROCESS, WHEN PROPERLY LIMITED, ONLY TAKES A FEW HOURS, AND WE IMMEDIATELY MOVE
11660
ON TO THE DIGGING. I MAN THE TRANSIT AND DIRECT THE DEPTHS AND PLACEMENT OF THE CUTS. MAC AND I INTERPRET THE EARTH AS WE GO, REACHING DOWN TO
01050
THE PROPER BEARING SOIL, DEVELOPING PLANS TO
02010
DEAL WITH SUBSURFACE SPRINGS, LAYERS OF CLAY, AND HIDDEN PROBLEMS OF ALL KINDS UNTIL WE HAVE CARVED AWAY A PROPER BUILDING PAD. WE ARE ALMOST ALWAYS DIGGING ON A STEEP HILLSIDE, SO
02100
THESE PADS STEP DOWN THE SLOPE IN TERRACES. IT IS A ONE-WAY PROCESS, STARTING AT THE TOP. THE MACHINE CAN'T CRAWL BACK UP TO THE PREVIOUS TERRACE, SO WE HAVE TO PLAN THE PROCESS STRATEGICALLY AND GET IT RIGHT THE FIRST TIME. IF IT WERE DONE WRONG, THE BULLDOZER WOULD HAVE TO TRAVEL BACK AROUND THROUGH THE TREES TO PERFORM CORRECTIVE WORK AT A HIGHER LEVEL, UNDOING ALL OF OUR CARE IN THE CLEARING PROCESS.

THE EXCAVATED EARTH IS CAREFULLY STACKED CLOSE TO EACH EDGE WHERE BACKFILL WILL BE NEEDED ONCE THE FOUNDATION IS COMPLETE. WE STOCKPILE JUST ENOUGH DIRT AT ALL EDGES SO THAT WE CAN MINIMIZE THE HAULING OF DIRT AND USE OF MACHINES AROUND THE PERIMETER. LATER WE WILL RUN CONCRETE PUMPS, MIXERS, AND BOOM TRUCKS EXCLUSIVELY WITHIN THE FOUNDATION AND THE NARROW ACCESS DRIVEWAY. THE HOUSE WILL BE CONSTRUCTED IN A HORIZONTAL SEQUENCE OF ASSEMBLY FROM THE BACK OF THE SITE OUT, RATHER THAN THE NORMAL VERTICAL SEQUENCE OF ONE FLOOR AT A TIME. THIS ALLOWS US TO BRING THE MACHINERY CLOSE TO THE WORK, WITHOUT BUILDING AN ACCESS ROAD OUTSIDE THE FOUNDA-
01043
TION. CAREFUL CONSTRUCTION SEQUENCING IS ESSENTIAL IN SETTING A PROJECT INTO ITS ENVIRONMENT. IF WE DIDN'T DO THE CONSTRUCTION THIS WAY, THE SPACE OF THE HOUSE, AND ITS EXPERIENCE, WOULD BE COMPLETELY DIFFERENT.

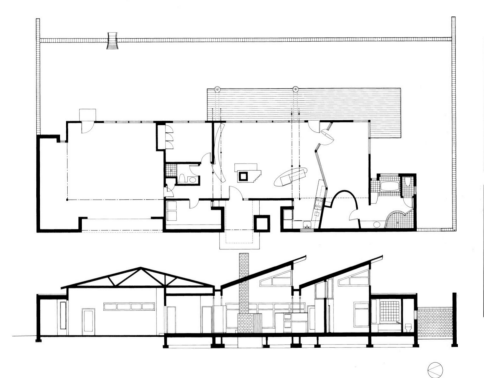

3 WARPING TO THE SITE

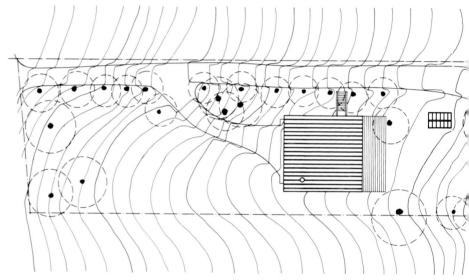

GIG HARBOR, WASHINGTON 1993

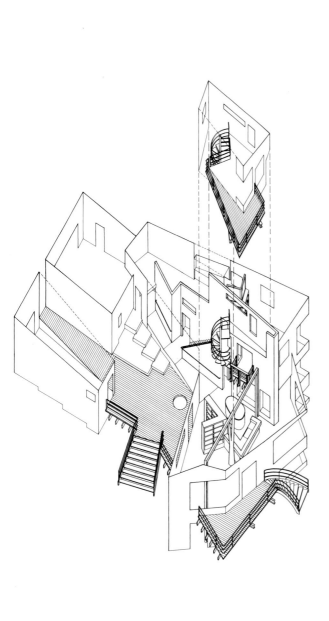

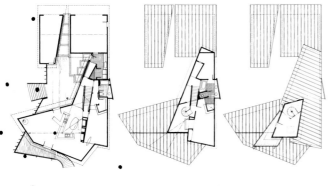

FOUNDATIONS

When we built a new house on Puget Sound for our parents in 1993 it was a collaborative project, with our mother and father and both of us working together closely throughout the entire process. We have built a number of things together as a family. From very early in our lives, there were always projects like tree houses, furniture, and small objects. The family's first major building project was the cabin we all built together during the 1970's on Harstine Island, in southern Puget Sound. This started when our sister, Kristen, and we were in junior high and high school. The cabin took several years of summers, weekends, and vacations to complete.

01043

In building the cabin, we decided to use only hand tools and did not bring electric power to the property until after it was nearly completed, which probably didn't help our already slow, learn-as-we-go time schedule. On the other hand, in many ways this is where we started intimately appreciating the characteristics of wood. When every cut is done with handsaws, all holes are made with a bit and brace, and when every notch is shaped with hammer and chisel, you really get to know the properties of materials and tools. The cabin had a lot of heavy timbers and large pieces of wood, so there were many long sawing operations. We also learned a lot about concrete, as the cabin was built up on concrete columns, floating above the ground to leave the natural grades and vegetation as undisturbed as possible.

06100

For the new house, even prior to finding property and designing the house for my parents, we had already purchased most of the windows we would use from the boneyard of an old-time Tacoma millwork manufacturer. These robust wooden windows, manufactured to the wrong dimensions, had been built for but never used in the restoration of the Longmire Lodge at Mount Rainier—a building we knew well, since we had lived at the foot of the mountain as children and often picnicked and hiked there. These windows became an important determinant of the dimensions, millwork details, and overall look and feel of the house.

06200

TOOLS

OUR FATHER'S FATHER WAS A STONE CUTTER, PRIMARILY WORKING ON GRANITE MONUMENTS IN MINNESOTA AND SOUTH DAKOTA, FROM THE '20S THROUGH ABOUT 1960. MY FATHER GREW UP AROUND THIS WORK, OFTEN HELPING TO DELIVER AND SET MONUMENTS. AT ONE POINT MY GRANDFATHER WAS PART OWNER OF A SMALL GRANITE QUARRY, WHICH WENT OUT OF BUSINESS DURING THE DEPRESSION. WE WERE CONSEQUENTLY ALWAYS VERY RESPECTFUL OF GRANITE AND THE CRAFT OF WORKING WITH MATERIALS OF ANY KIND. MY FATHER INHERITED HIS FATHER'S TOOLS, INCLUDING STONE, WOODWORKING, AND MECHANICS' TOOLS, AND THESE ARE THE TOOLS THAT WE GREW UP WITH AND USED FOR BUILDING FURNITURE AND TOYS AND CHRISTMAS PRESENTS, WORKING WITH OUR DAD. HE AND MARK AND I STILL USE MANY OF THESE TOOLS NOW, AND THE TWISTED TWO-HEADED WRENCH, WHICH HAS ALWAYS BEEN OUR FAVORITE, HAS BEEN FOR MANY YEARS THE UNIQUELY APPROPRIATE LOGO FOR ANDERSON ANDERSON ARCHITECTURE.

ANOTHER IMPORTANT ELEMENT, WHICH CAME TO US FROM OUR MOTHER'S SIDE OF THE FAMILY, IS A BLACK STEEL COOKING UTENSIL USED FOR MAKING A SPECIAL NORWEGIAN CHRISTMAS COOKIE CALLED KRUMKAKKE. THIS IRON HAS BEEN IN THE FAMILY FOR A VERY LONG TIME. NO ONE REALLY KNOWS HOW OLD IT IS, BUT THE STORY IS THAT OUR GREAT-GRANDMOTHER CARRIED IT ON THE BOAT OVER FROM NORWAY TO THE UNITED STATES WHEN SHE AND HER PARENTS IMMIGRATED, PROBABLY IN THE 1860S. SHE WAS ABOUT FIVE YEARS OLD AT THE TIME, AND THIS WAS THE ONLY OBJECT IN HER CHARGE TO CARRY DURING THE OCEAN CROSSING. IN THE NEW HOUSE WE MADE A SPECIAL PLACE FOR THIS FAMILY HEIRLOOM, HANGING IT ON A GIANT HOOK ON THE STEEL COLUMN IN THE KITCHEN. THE WISHBONE FORM OF THIS TOOL HELPED TO GENERATE A NUMBER OF IDEAS AND STRUCTURAL ELEMENTS IN THE HOUSE AND HAS CONTINUED AS AN IMPORTANT IDEA IN NUMEROUS DRAWINGS, PRINTS, AND SUBSEQUENT BUILDING PROJECTS.

08000

There were a great many other "found" influences on the eventual form of the house. The property came with a nicely proportioned but fatally worm-eaten small bungalow built about 1900, which had to be demolished to build the new house. We felt a great deal of history on the site and heard a lot of stories from neighbors who knew "Old Man Samuelson," in whose family the house had remained from construction. Over the many years this family had been there they had done much to the property, with rock walls, outbuildings, fruit trees, flowers, and plants of all kinds scattered amidst the natural vegetation and very old trees.

We always talked about winding this house into the site, since we were working around so many preexisting forces. This project was very different from our usual experience of building new houses on previously untouched ground, and we felt a great responsibility to respect the site. A circle of very old, very big fir trees formed a neat ring around the old house. These were also to cradle the new house, and we took care to protect them by largely confining the new construction to the existing excavations of the old house. Now views from the house and trails to the beach wind through and between these trees. They block the harsh afternoon summer sun but are limbed up to bring in the brief vital periods of morning and late-day sun present for much of the year. These trees create a kind of natural courtyard on the property, and the form of the house follows this direction to provide additional layers of exterior and interior spaces enclosed within. The entry courtyard is wrapped on three sides by the building and by trees on the fourth. Its south and west exposure is sheltered from the wind but open to views and late afternoon light, making it a much-used outdoor living space on otherwise cool and breezy days.

TIME AND MATERIALS

WE BUILT THIS HOUSE AFTER BUILDING A LOT OF OTHER HOUSES. WHILE MANY ARCHITECTS START WITH A HOUSE FOR THEIR PARENTS, THIS WAS NOT THE CASE FOR US. SOME OF OUR OTHER HOUSES ARE MORE EXPERIMENTAL. FOR OUR PARENTS' HOUSE, WE WORKED WITH A PALETTE OF PROCESSES AND MATERIALS THAT WERE VERY FAMILIAR, GIVING INCREASED FOCUS TO THE LEVEL OF TEXTURAL RICHNESS AND SPATIAL INTEGRATION WE DESIRED.

IN THE NORTHWEST, AMPLIFIED ON THIS WATERFRONT SITE, IT IS OFTEN DAMP AND COOL. THIS IS ONE REASON WE HAVE USED SO MUCH EXPOSED NATURAL WOOD INSIDE. CHOSEN FROM NATIVE TREES OF THE NORTHWEST, EACH WOOD HAS BEEN USED IN A LOCATION THAT EXPLOITS ITS BEST PROPERTIES. OUR GROWING INTEREST IN THE WAY MATERIALS AGE WITH TIME AND USE HAS INFORMED THIS SELECTION, KNOWING WE AND OUR PARENTS WOULD BE SEEING THE MATERIALS CLOSE-UP OVER A LONG PERIOD.

ALL EXPOSED INTERIOR WOOD SURFACES ARE TREATED WITH NON-COLORED PENETRATING OILS—NO HARD FINISHES, NO STAINS, NO BLEACHES. THE OILS BRING OUT THE RICHNESS OF THE WOOD AND GIVE A LUSTER THAT DEEPENS WITH AGE. SOME PEOPLE THINK THAT HARD FINISHES PROTECT WOOD MORE, BUT WE FEEL THAT POLYURETHANE FINISHES SEAL YOU AWAY FROM A DIRECT EXPERIENCE OF THE MATERIAL, LIKE TRYING TO TOUCH SOMETHING THROUGH A LAYER OF PLEXIGLAS. WITH AN OILED FINISH YOU CAN TOUCH THE EVER-CHANGING WOOD ITSELF.

At the very center of the house is a forked tree column. This tree is important to us, because it is the only tree that was cut in order to make way for the house. We took this decision very seriously, trying hard to avoid having to cut it. Eventually we decided to place the tree as the central support in the main interior space, carrying the load of the tower and the light well above. It is a very special tree—a Port Orford cedar—which is a relatively rare native Northwest tree highly prized by boat builders for the beauty and flexible strength of its wood.

The house that surrounds this tree is open, with few rooms defined in a typical way by doors. The main floor of the house is zoned in part by a stepped progression through service areas leading between the garage and kitchen. Ramped floors link the levels and allow the house to adapt to the sloping topography. The living room, dining room, and kitchen areas are all under one big, tent-like roof, partitioned somewhat by the forked shelving/cabinet walls in the middle of the room. This openness allows the light captured by the tower element to flood down through all three stories of the middle part of the house, illuminating the interplay of floating roof planes. The kitchen and dining areas are the most central spaces, with the dining table next to the window, privileged with the best views of Mount Rainier to the east and the sweep of Puget Sound to the south and west. There is only this one place to eat in the house, and this table is the focal point of many extended meals and family gatherings at all times of the day.

PREVIOUS PAGES: FABRICATION OF
CURVED EXTERIOR STEEL STAIRCASE
FOR ANDERSON HOUSE.

4   SAGGING ROOFS AND DROOPING FLOORS

The Tonn, Enlow, and Obata houses represent projects that have allowed us to strengthen the ways in which many of our diverse thoughts about nature, construction systems, and spatial experience can be brought together as integrated ambitions. These three projects clarify many of the ideas and influences of our earlier construction work—they share many concepts, approaches, and details, and build upon one another as a series of ideas.

We have designed a number of projects for the Obata Corporation, a civil infrastructure construction contractor in Shizuoka, Japan, with a growing sideline business in residential building. Our involvement in the Japanese construction industry stems from Japanese economic interest in the American construction industry, mainly the rational standardization and integrated product systems that make wood construction more affordable in America than in Japan. Within this window of opportunity, our particular focus in Japan has been in using standardized construction systems as a rational tool for site-specific concerns.

Even prior to visiting or working in Japan, we were strongly influenced and inspired by traditional and modern Japanese architecture. Some of this influence has been direct, and some of it has come to us filtered through the Japanese-influenced work of modern domestic architecture in California, Oregon, and Washington. The craft of traditional and modern wood architecture is an important sidelight to this interest. Primarily, though, we are interested in the Japanese integration of interior and exterior space, or more broadly, the integration of natural and constructed space.

OBATA HOUSE AND OFFICES

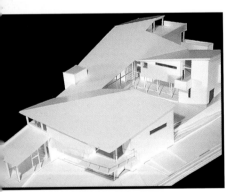

Hiromitsu Obata asked us to design a building that would be primarily a large house for his family, but that would also include guest quarters for his business, and substantial office, parking, and storage spaces for the housing division of his family company. Although we planned to prefabricate some of the elements in the United States—and the project involved a number of relatively experimental construction systems—this design was dominated by complex accommodations to the constraints and opportunities of the site and program.

The land itself has been in the Obata family for generations. It is a long, narrow strip of land with a substantial cross-slope, wedged into a typical Japanese neighborhood of densely mixed houses, apartment buildings, offices, and industrial facilities. The Obata Corporation offices and warehouses are across the street. Additional contiguous land owned by Obata is intended for speculative housing development. We have designed the master plan for the entire site, as well as several adjacent houses and other buildings.

In contemporary Japan, building sites are generally prepared as large, organized civil construction projects in advance of the design of individual buildings to be placed on the sites. The typically hilly terrain is terraced into a flat, structurally compacted building site, with little of the traditional Japanese sensitivity for landscape and nature. We are always pointing out this contradiction to our clients and attempting to have some influence on the earthwork before the damage is done. Large earthwork projects of this sort are actually the bread and butter of the Obata Corporation. On the other hand, working with them, we have direct communication with the bulldozers and a good deal of influence on the land planning. In the design for Obata's own house and offices, we have worked very hard to drape the building sensitively across the natural slope of the property.

Another important factor in designing buildings in Japan has been the national building code requirements, which restrict the blocking of sunlight, or casting of shadows, from one property to another. One of the first steps in the design process is the calculation and three-dimensional mapping of the project's maximum solar envelope, so as to maintain sunlight on neighboring properties. Associated architects in Japan sometimes supply these diagrams to us; however, our office has always learned to work through these complex calculations. Often, these solar envelope drawings are more interesting than the buildings themselves.

The Obata house and office is formed to create three courtyards opening to the south and east. The interior space pushes largely closed walls against the north and west edges of the property, focusing instead on the courtyards, with optimized exposure to sunlight and views. The most open of these courts, facing the principal street, is a public entry, parking, and staging area for the business offices. The northwest court is the play area, service court, and private parking area for the residence. The central court, which is the most emphatically pure figure in the building, is the primary space of the house, to which all other areas, definitions, and geometries defer, and yet even this courtyard is skewed slightly to accommodate the contextual complexities of the site. Outside of this central figure, the building is a fluid series of impure, interpenetrating spaces balancing the internal demands of their respective functions with the equally pressing demands of adjacent spaces and the shared ambitions for light, view, air, and a continuity of space. The open, interior space of the house is unified by its clear relationship to the figural courtyard. The floor planes echo the downward slope of the land, as does the undulating roof, flowing continuously and independently over the house, within the invisible solar envelope established by the building code.

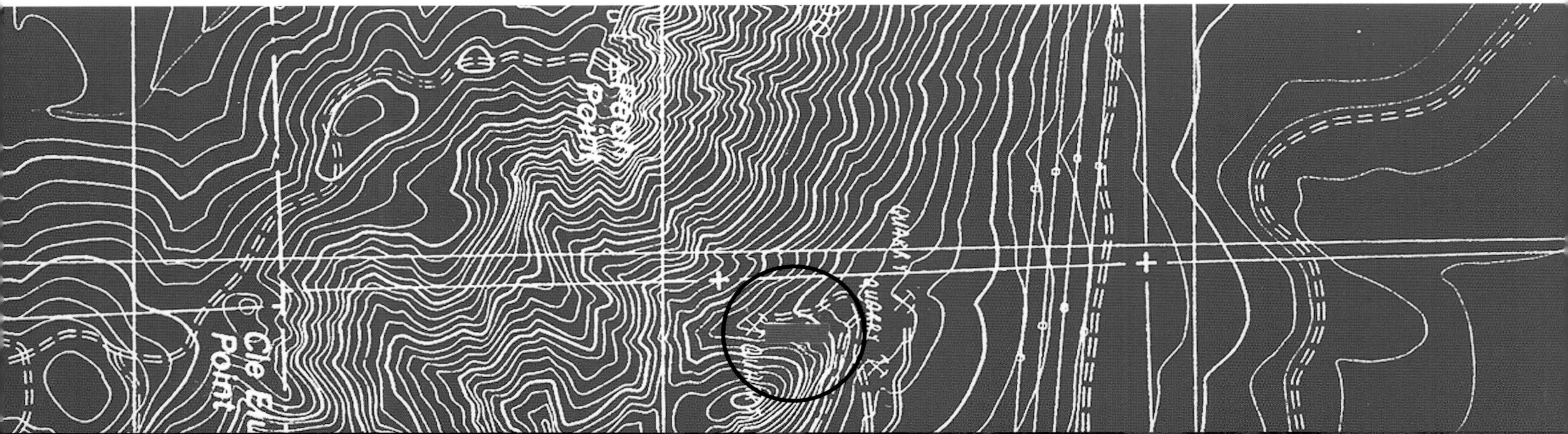

QUARRY

QUARRY

QUARRY

Peah
Point

Cle Elu
Point

ENLOW MOUNTAIN CABIN

CLE ELUM, WASHINGTON 1998

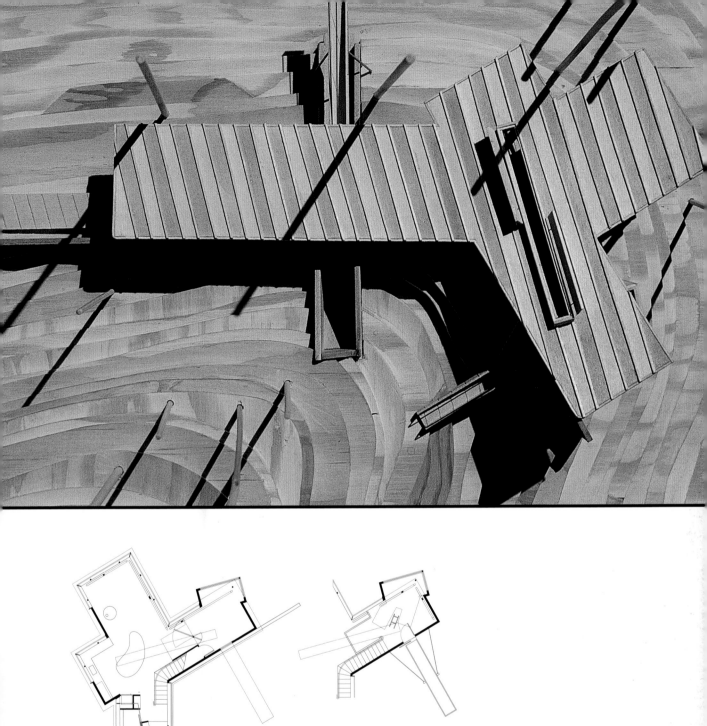
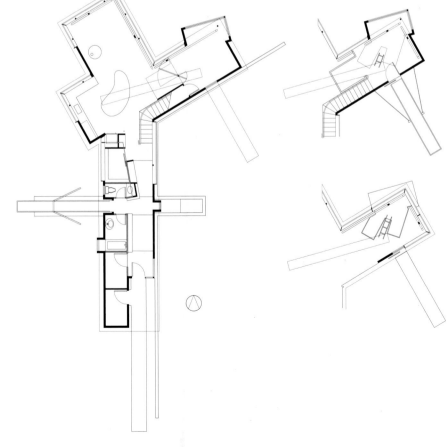

In late spring, the lower parts of the trail to the Enlow mountain cabin are muddy with runoff from melting snow at higher elevations. Beginning at the galvanized steel gate in the thick forest of mixed pine and fir peculiar to this eastern face of the Cascade Mountains, we climb up towards the light above, the air becoming noticeably warmer and drier as we go. The house is first viewed from the road below as an uncertain attachment to the distant rock face just above the tree line of the looming mountain above. Climbing higher, the house is viewed intermittently between the trees and across the canyon at occasional points along the 1,000-foot vertical climb.

Reaching a high meadow, we turn back sharply towards the view and the continuing upward trail. Far ahead, blocking the narrow end of the trail, we see the pinched front door of the new house, perched precariously on an L-shaped ledge at the northeast point of the canyon.

Arriving at the house, the journey continues up a steel-grate ramp to the front door and then descends within the house along a wooden, sloping path, beneath a plywood ceiling that rises upward toward the journey's first panoramic view of the river valley and the North Cascades. At the foot of the interior ramp, the building forks towards competing views. A stair follows the cliff wall upward to a small loft, and from there a door leads onto a bridge back to the next ledge: the house is a switchback in the continuing climb to the top of the mountain above. An interior ladder rises through the crotch of a fork-shaped loft to reach the two-faced, 360-degree outlook for the family's twin sons.

The roof is designed to drop all snow to the downslope side of the house with structure and steel roofing panels following the optimal fall line. Since the primary exposure faces north, the roof rises to accommodate south light and towering cliff views along the upper wall cut deep into the rock. The house sits at the point of the ridge to shed run-off downward along both legs of the retaining wall. A concrete chute at the midpoint of the long leg of the wall allows accumulating snow and rock to be funneled beneath the house. A small lookout on the west wall of the house pokes out beyond the trees affording a clear view up and down the canyon.

The house is constructed of stressed-skin sandwich panels built within the resistant enclosure of an engineered concrete retaining wall cut into the rock. The siding, chosen for minimal maintenance, consists of cement board panels alternately left natural gray or stained transparent green as a sort of geometric camouflage against the rock and sparse vegetation of the cliff. The siding pattern follows the fall line established in alternating gray-painted and galvanized steel roof panels. This same banding continues subtly on the interior with panels of A-face Douglas Fir plywood installed as continuous loops across floor, ceiling, and walls. Diagonal steel struts brace the window walls with aluminum-sash glazing that floats just outside the structural wall plane.

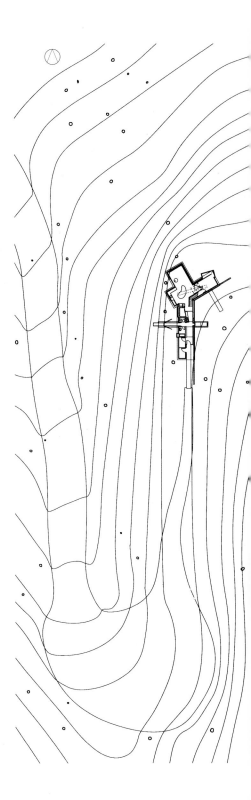

TONN RESIDENCE

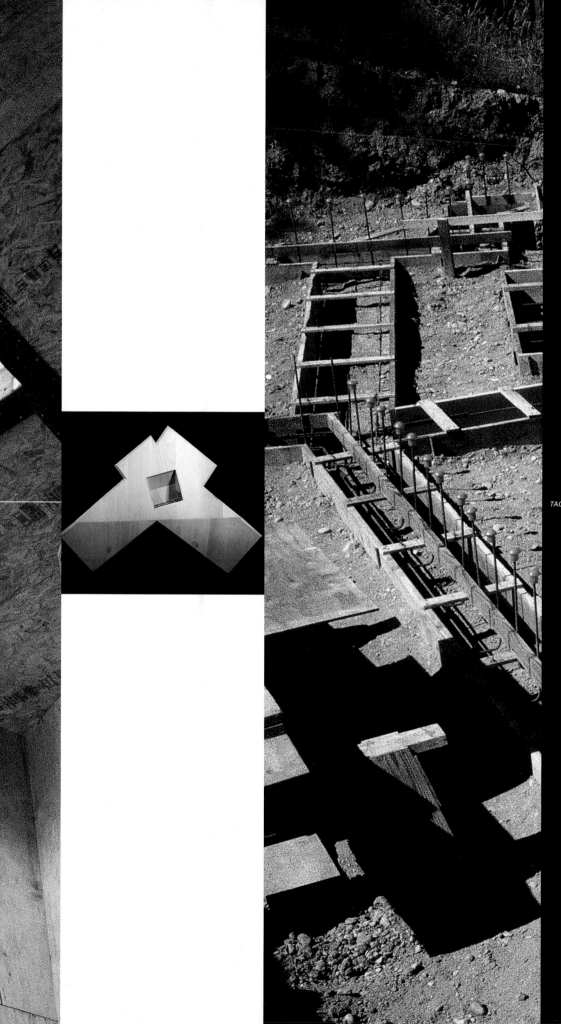

TACOMA, WASHINGTON 2000

UPPER FLOOR

MAIN FLOOR

GROUND FLOOR

EARTH AND SKY

The Tonn house, on a high bank above Puget Sound, has a T-shaped organization of interior spaces, arranged to form an entry court at the back of the house and a partially contained living deck on the view side of the house facing northwest (the first sites to be built on in the Pacific Northwest were usually waterfront or view sites facing south, commanding the best views and the best sunlight. These prime sites are now rare, and, in addition, they miss out on the spectacular views to the northwest, where the summer sun sets behind the Olympic mountain range). Achieving a northwest view at the Tonn site required turning the major sweep of glass away from the sun. We often confront this need to balance views in one direction, sunlight in another, while at the same time minimizing the total amount of glass area. The strict energy codes of the Northwest limit the area of glass for a given amount of floor space and favor distribution of the glass to the south face of the building. While admittedly well intentioned, these overly simplistic formulas profoundly affect any architectural approach to light and views. They also interfere with issues such as minimizing heat loss and drafty discomfort, maximizing positive solar gain and daylighting, conserving energy, and making a bright, happy place to live. These are tricky problems—there are many others as well, such as rain, or groundwater, or the slipping earth itself, which frequently require a good deal of twisting—conceptual and physical—in order to create some positive balance between the competing forces.

The Tonn house is a literal example of conservative, practical twisting. The basic concept and structure of the house are simple. Prior to dropping into some accommodation with its site, the house is conceived as a rectilinear organization of spaces and straightforward structural components. The rooms—or more accurately, since the house is primarily one big continuous room, the defined areas with specific functions such as cooking and dining and sleeping and reading—are organized according to their most favorable relationships to the sun and views. The kitchen is given morning light from the east, for example, and a central position in relation to all the light and views and functions in the house. The dining room faces the sunset and mountains. The sunroom faces south. This is the first pass of organization in the particularization of the site. If access to the light or the view, or avoidance of a cliff or a particular tree, or the blockage of a particular water-

DOORS AND WINDOWS

08000

OUR HOUSES ARE ALWAYS DISTORTED BY THEIR WINDOWS. BASICALLY, WE WORK WITH THREE KINDS OF WINDOWS: CONTINUOUS SWEEPS OF

13600

GLASS OPENING UP THE VIEW AND SUCKING IN SUNLIGHT OR AT LEAST THE FILTERED BRIGHTNESS OF SOUTHERN MISTS; INCIDENTAL WINDOWS FLOATING PRAGMATICALLY ALONG BLANK, CLOSED WALLS; AND WINDOWS OF SPECIFIC PERSONALITY, USUALLY METAL CLAD BOXES

11660

AIMED LIKE WANDERING EYES, TO CREATE A PARTICULAR SPACE, TO FRAME A FAVORED VIEW, AND TO MAKE A FACE. THERE ARE ALSO INTERIOR WINDOWS. THESE HAVE TWO RELATED PURPOSES: TO SPREAD

01060

LIGHT DEEP INTO THE RECESSES OF THE BUILDING ALONG THE PLANE OF THE CEILING, AND TO ALLOW THE CONTINUOUS PLANE OF THE CEILING TO DEFINE A SWEEPING, BENDING SPACE INDEPENDENT OF THE INTERIOR WALLS AND FIXTURES.

08000

RECENTLY WE HAVE BEEN EXPERIMENTING WITH OUR OWN CURTAINWALL SYSTEMS. MOST OF WHAT WE KNOW ABOUT THE REAL ART AND

08610

TECHNOLOGY OF WINDOWS WE LEARNED FROM PEOPLE AT COAST CRAFT MANUFACTURING, AN OLD CUSTOM MILLWORK FABRICATOR IN TACOMA. THEY HAD THESE GREAT SAWTOOTH-ROOFED SHOPS AND WAREHOUSES ON THE TIDEFLATS IN TACOMA, AND THEY HAD SOME GREAT CRAFTSPEOPLE. NOW THEY ARE OUT OF BUSINESS, PARTLY BECAUSE THEIR OLD-FASHIONED PRACTICES WERE EXPENSIVE, FRUSTRATING, AND SLOW. BUT WE LEARNED A GREAT DEAL FROM THEM DURING THE LAST TEN YEARS OF THEIR HUNDRED-YEAR RUN.

THE TONN AND ENLOW HOUSES USE AN EVOLVING ADAPTATION OF A HYBRID ALUMINUM AND TIMBER FRAME CURTAIN WALL SYSTEM THAT WE FIRST DEVELOPED ON THE KENNEDY HOUSE, WHERE WE WERE INSTALLING LARGE EXPANSES OF GLASS WALL ON A VERY TIGHT CON-

08000

STRUCTION BUDGET. THE SYSTEM ON THE TONN AND ENLOW HOUSES

08000

INVOLVES APPLYING STANDARD ALUMINUM WINDOW UNITS ATTACHED TO A FRAME OF WOOD MEMBERS THAT ARE SIMULTANEOUSLY LOADBEARING STRUCTURAL ELEMENTS HOLDING UP THE ROOF AND FINISHED, EXPOSED WINDOW MULLIONS. THERE ARE THREE LEVELS OF

06100

WOOD STRUCTURE MAKING UP THE SYSTEM WITH THE ALUMINUM FRAME WINDOWS FLOATING FREELY ON THE OUTSIDE. EACH LEVEL OF STRUCTURE IS SET ON AN INDEPENDENT GRID TO CREATE AN APPARENTLY CASUAL RELATIONSHIP IN THE ADJACENCY OF THE FRAME, SUGGESTING A SYSTEM IN MOTION. THE DEPTH AND MISALIGNMENT OF THIS FRAME STRUCTURE DEVELOP LAYERS OF SPACE AND A NETWORK OF HIGHLIGHTS AND SHADOWS CAPTURED IN THE BASKETWORK OF WOOD AND GLASS. IN THIS WAY WE HAVE A COMPLETELY OPEN GLASS WALL, WHICH FILTERS THE TRANSPARENT SPACE THROUGH A WARM, PROTECTIVE SCREEN OF TIMBERS AND STICKS, CREATING AN EXPERIENCE OF THE LIGHT AND VIEW SIMILAR TO PEERING OUT INTO A CLEARING OR BEACH FROM BEHIND A THIN STAND OF FIR TREES.

course suggests the twisting of the house here and there, then we twist specific elements—respecting the idealized structural order and maintaining a generally affordable and explainable means of construction.

There is also the slope of the land. We used to think that the land was quite separate from the issue of the sky's relationship to the roof. Now we think of the roof and land all together. The Tonn house is about the earth and the sky.

The house is on a fairly steep, dish-shaped slope falling down toward Puget Sound and looking across to Vashon Island. The surrounding trees accentuate the inward focus of the slightly dished slope, so that the house appears to sit in a fairly distinct trough, following the fall line of the hill. We bent the roof of the house into a shallow "V" paralleling the cross-slope dish of the hillside. At the same time, we dropped the longitudinal axis of the roof fold downward to follow the primary slope of the hill. The house slumps into a comfortable resting position on the earth, not statically resisting its position, but flowing into the implied motion of the site.

The roof is the most important element of this house. Its logic is not primarily related to an exterior visual coherence with the hill. The primary interest for us is never what the building looks like from the outside. We are most interested in the spatial experience of the interior, and the spatial experience of the adjacent exterior spaces that are shaped by the interior. This roof is most important to us as a heavy warm cedar cloud weighing in on the interior and defining a specific space between the sloping land and the heavy sky. This is a characteristic Northwest experience: living on a hillside under a heavy cloud. It is gentle and comforting, if in a sometimes smothering kind of way. Light pokes in horizontally at sunrise and sunset, creating spectacular moments at the horizon, reflecting richly off the ceiling of clouds. Sometimes during the day a hole opens up and the light pours in from the middle of the sky. This is the way the roof works in the Tonn house, with its central dormer angling toward the southeastern sky, bringing light over the shoulder of the house, into the kitchen, and deep down through the center of the house. This is a continuing development of the approach to daylight used in our earlier houses.

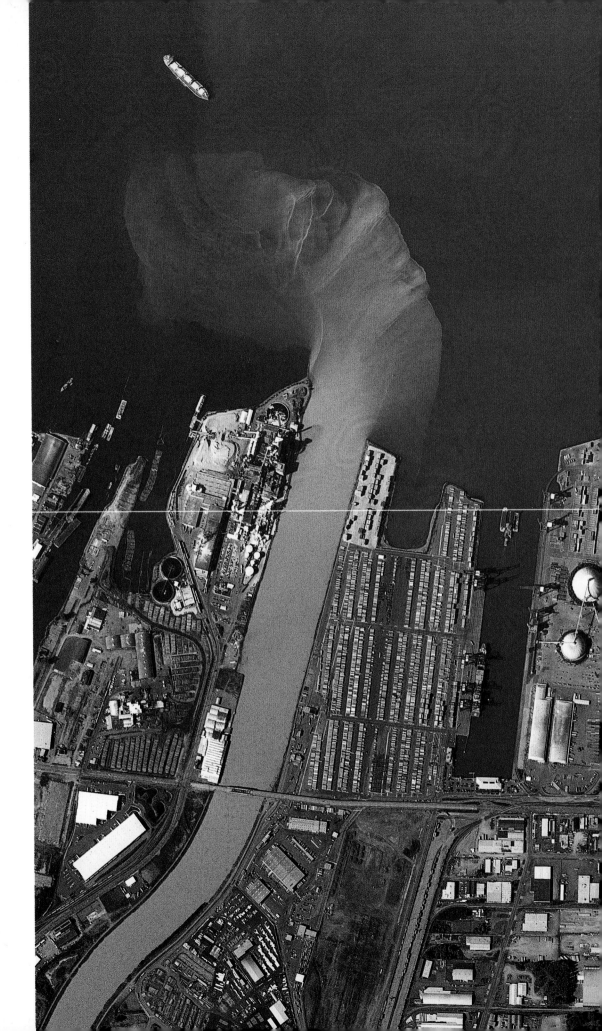

06 **FRAMING** 100

THE TIDEFLATS

We grew up in Tacoma, Washington. Its always been a slightly off-the-mark, smoke-belching, down-on-its-luck industrial city with one of the most beautiful and active deep-water ports in America. In the 1880s, before what Tacomans like to think of as underhanded business skullduggery brought the transcontinental railroad terminus to Seattle instead of Tacoma, this was considered the City of Destiny. This motto is still invoked in daily business conversation, with an always conscious but never quite clearly apportioned mixture of industrial age irony and Pacific Century ambition.

The city's industrial zone 01600 and dock facilities sit on the delta of the Puyallup River which spills a rich, muddy brown flume into the clear blue depths of Puget Sound. This area is called the Tideflats.

Mount Rainier, at 14,442 feet (as every school child knows), 00230 looms above the tideflats with a scale and majesty unequalled from any other vantage point in the state. Usually it peeks out from behind some tall nearby hill or stand of trees, but from the Tideflats you look straight up the sea-level river valley and view the whole moun- 02900 tain from its base to the summit. The mountain has a tremendous presence in everyone's lives. It is always spoken of in strangely per- sonified, subconsciously spiritual terms. Nobody says, "I can see the mountain today." We say, "the mountain is out today," as though it clearly has a capricious will of its own. Which it does, always jumping out unexpectedly through some unlikely gap in the landscape to present itself in continuously transforming trans- parencies, luminosities, and cloud-fragmented formal configura- tions. Mount Rainier is rarely referred to by name. Locally it is called "The Mountain." The number of amazing mountains circling this city may make this singular reference seem strange to anyone who hasn't lived in its shadow for some time.

The Puyallup River begins life in the Puyallup and Tahoma Glaciers on the southwest shoulder of the mountain. Its two icy tributaries 15400 hook north and merge as a broad brown flow across a verdant, black-earth flood plain before branching into a fine network of rivulets cut into the tidal mudflats of Commencement Bay. At least that's what it used to do, as we know from one of the last remaining natural mudflats on Puget Sound, the Nisqually Delta, still flowing freely about 30 miles to the south. Soft, squishy, seaweed-smelling 02200 mudflats are fantastic. At low tide the mudflats in the Northwest can be immense, because of the large tidal variations, which average about 20 vertical feet. We have built a number of projects related to these pungent mudflats and their forking, flowing uncertainties.

The Tideflats in Tacoma still have lots of mud and a labyrinthine net- work of opportunistic waterways, but they are dredged, navigable, and abutted by shipyards, warehouses, container docks, and facto- ries. This network of steaming industry and transportation is beau- tiful too, and it is also the place where you can learn how to build anything, and learn how everything that gets built is linked into the flows of a complex, international, industrial ecology.

THE FRAMING SECTION IS ABOUT BUSINESS AND THE SYSTEMS INVOLVED IN MAKING THINGS. BUSINESS ENCOMPASSES ALL OF THE PRACTICAL ISSUES INVOLVED IN MAKING A LIVING, OR EVEN IN TRYING TO GET RICH, BUT WE THINK OF BUSINESS 00240 PRIMARI- LY AS THE INCREDIBLE COMMERCE OF INTERCONNEC- TIVITY INVOLVING SO MUCH OF THE WORLD'S PRO- DUCTIVITY AND AMBITION. ABSTRACT FLOWS OF CAPITAL EXCHANGE FASCINATE US, BUT WE ARE MOST INTERESTED IN BUSINESS AT MORE PHYSICAL LEVELS. IN THE BEGINNING, AND IN SOME WAYS STILL, BUSINESS FOR US IS ALL ABOUT TRUCKS— SHORT BOX, FLAT BED, LOW BOY, DUELLIE, LONG HAUL, SEMI, BOOM. A BOOM TRUCK IS REALLY AN ICON. MOTORS, WHEELS, TOOLS, TRAVEL, CONSTRUC- TION, SIGNS ON THE DOOR. THE WHOLE BUSINESS WRAPPED UP AS A TRUCK. STUDENTS, ESPECIALLY, ASK US WHY WE GOT STARTED IN THE CONSTRUCTION BUSINESS. THERE ARE A MILLION COMPONENTS TO SOME COMPREHENSIVE ANSWER: POLITICAL AND ETHICAL ISSUES, ECONOMIC STRATEGIES AND CUL- TURAL THEORIES, ACCIDENTS OF OPPORTUNITY, THOUGHTS ABOUT PROCESS AND THE ORIGINS OF IDEAS. SOME OF ALL THAT CAN BE REDUCED TO AN UNARTICULATED, STUBBORN CERTAINTY ABOUT THE RIGHT WAY TO MAKE THINGS. SOME UNDERSTAND- ING OF THE CRITICAL ARCHITECTURAL IMPORTANCE OF CONSTRUCTION AND COMMERCE CONTINUES TO ARRIVE WITH CLEARER INSIGHTS AND BROADER CON- CLUSIONS. BUT WHO WANTS TO TALK ABOUT THEO- RIES OF CONSTRUCTION? THE QUICKEST ANSWER IS ALSO THE TRUEST: "SO WE'D HAVE A GOOD EXCUSE TO BUY A TRUCK." YOU CANNOT UNDERSTAND THE ALLURE OF THE TIDEFLATS OR PACIFIC AVENUE WITH- OUT ALSO UNDERSTANDING THE ALLURE OF A TRUCK.

You can find just about anything on the Tideflats: truckers, pipefitters, tug and barge crews, loggers, engineers, welders, and expert craftspeople. There are container cranes, log booms, sparkling white hills of bauxite, red hot copper mill tailings steaming in the saltwater, scrap yards, batch plants, log mills, pulp mills, smelters, aerospace subcontractors, extruders, pull-truders, superfund clean-up sites, foundries, hot-dip galvanizers, sandblasters, powder coaters, steel fabricators, millwork and cabinet shops, smokestacks, freighters, railroads, firecrackers, tax-free cigarettes, and floating casinos.

THE NORTH ARROW AND THE SOUTH

THE SHADOW OF MOUNT RAINIER IS IMPORTANT, AS THE MOUNTAIN LIES TO THE SOUTH OF TACOMA. SOUTH IS OUR MOST IMPORTANT DIRECTION BY FAR. IF YOU WANT TO UNDERSTAND ANYTHING ABOUT HOW WE GO ABOUT BUILDING, YOU HAVE TO LOOK SOUTH.

WE'RE ALWAYS ASKING STUDENTS, "WHERE'S THE NORTH ARROW? WHERE'S THE NORTH ARROW? ITS NOT SOME DECORATION AT THE END OF THE DRAWING TO PLEASE YOUR TEACHERS. HOW CAN YOU DRAW EVEN ONE LINE ON THE PAGE WITHOUT A NORTH ARROW?" WHY IS IT ALWAYS A NORTH ARROW? THIS IS PART OF THE DISTANCING PROBLEM OF DIAGRAMS, SYMBOLS, AND LANGUAGE: ONE ADDITIONAL REMOVAL FROM A VISCERAL UNDERSTANDING OF SPACE AND THE PRIMARY ELEMENTS. IN JAPAN, IT IS NOT UNUSUAL TO ORIENT DRAWINGS TO THE SOUTH. THIS IS MORE SENSIBLE FOR THOSE OF US IN THE NORTHERN HEMISPHERE. REALLY, IT IS THE SOUTH THAT WE'RE INTERESTED IN. WE LOOK AT THE NORTH ARROW TO FIGURE OUT WHICH WAY IS SOUTH. IN THE NORTHWEST, THE SUN IS EVERYTHING TO US. WE RARELY SEE IT. THE RAIN SWEEPS UP FROM THE SOUTHWEST. FOG ROLLS UP BETWEEN THE ISLANDS TO THE SOUTH. SOUTH HAS TO WIND INTO A SITE AROUND MANY TREES AND HILLS AND OBSTACLES. THE SOUTH WINDS INTO CITIES IN WAYS EQUALLY COMPLEX. THE COMPASS WON'T ALWAYS TELL YOU WHICH WAY THE LIGHT WILL REALLY ARRIVE AT ANY ONE SPECIFIC PLACE. PERHAPS THE NORTH ARROW MAKES SENSE THOUGH, AS A DIAGRAM. HOW COULD YOU REDUCE THE SOUTH TO A DIAGRAM? THE COLD, ANALYTIC NORTH ARROW STANDS AT THE TOP OF THE PAGE AS A WARNING. THEN WE CAN DRAW DOWN THE PAGE, FEELING OUR WAY INWARD TOWARDS OUR BODIES, TOWARDS THE SOUTH.

Our office now is on the waterfront of Elliot Bay in downtown Seattle, and our windows look out onto the immense cranes and industrial port facilities at the mouth of the Duwamish River. You can probably get anything you want there, too, but the place is tighter, more narrowly organized, and far less diverse. There isn't much room for us to operate, and we have the impression that if you want something made you have to start out already sure of what you want. That's a pretty weak way to be an architect— clear-headed, self-certain, and narrow-minded—so we often still take our projects down onto the Tideflats in Tacoma. That's where we got started in the business, knowing that we knew nothing at all. Of course we always start with some idea of what we're trying to do, but then we set things into motion and ski along with the flow of who-knows-who, who-knows-what, and how can we do something we don't already know using the limited time and money available. This is building as a learning process, rather than a specifying and ordering process.

Take the process of building stairs, for example. At best, stairs are fairly complicated, but architects, ourselves included, always seem to make them into the central headache of any project. When we build steel stairs we often try something new—it may involve rolling structural members into compound curves, or brake-forming steel plates into particular folds. Once we have found someone who can roll a certain curve, we may subsequently be advised that this part will no longer fit in any local galvanizing tank, and then we will have to rethink the possibilities for breaking the project down into some other configuration of smaller components. It is hard to enumerate the variables in a small project like this. Discussions with various shops always lead to a number of side loops, alternative possibilities, and the need to contact some other shop. Most of this kind of work can happen on the Tideflats, but sometimes we have to ship parts to Seattle or Portland, because a shipyard has the special equipment required to bend a specific part. There are many fabricators, and each one has some particular piece of machinery or experience, or an ingenious insight about some key component of the process, so the bids and the advice may vary widely.

The process isn't to draw something, bid it out, and then take the lowest bidder. That method is far too expensive for most of our projects. And anyway, it would be like trying to design something in a black box with little knowledge going into the project, and little more knowledge gained by the end.

Instead, we drive down to the Tideflats, start with someone we've worked with before, sketch the general parameters of the project, and then follow leads from one fabricator to another. We look at one machine and another and talk to one mechanic and another until we have refined our idea to fit a particular set of people and machines and ideas.

It is easy to understand the argument that architects don't have time to chase around industrial yards designing production details with machinists. On the other hand, if the architect isn't doing this phase of the design work, then a contractor or an industry salesperson is doing it. At a minimum, architects need to understand how all of these decision-making processes work. The more intriguing possibility is to move architects into the depths of industrial processes and the systems of production, while at the same time drawing upward the creative ingenuity and experience of the mechanics themselves.

WHEN WE WERE LITTLE WE SPENT A LOT OF TIME ON THE TIDEFLATS WITH OUR FAMILY [02070] **AT A SHIP DISMANTLER'S WAREHOUSE. THEY CUT UP OLD NAVY SHIPS AND FREIGHTERS AND SOLD OFF THE SCRAP. THE MOST INTERESTING STUFF—LIKE HATCH COVERS AND PORTHOLES AND NAVIGATION LIGHTS AND RADIO PARTS AND INDECIPHERABLE BRONZE FITTINGS—WAS SOLD OUT OF A HUGE, OLD, SIDEWAYS-LEANING, WOODEN WAREHOUSE. WE WOULD TAKE HOME ALL KINDS OF GREAT STUFF AND BUILD IT INTO SOMETHING NEW.**

NOW THE SHIP DISMANTLING BUSINESS HAS MOVED TO KOREA. [02070] **BUT THERE IS AN EVEN COOLER PLACE TO HANG OUT AND FIND SURPRISING STUFF. BOEING SURPLUS HAS ACRES OF EVEN MORE INDECIPHERABLE PARTS, LIKE STAINLESS STEEL SHEETS, BLOCKS OF ALUMINUM, COMPOSITE STRESS-SKIN PANELS, CABLE, RUBBER, PLASTICS, VIDEO PROJECTORS, SPRINGS, HOSES, PIPES, PUMPS, VALVES, AND ELECTRONIC INSTRUMENTS. ALMOST EVERYTHING WE HAVE BUILT HAS INVOLVED SOME BOEING PARTS. PEOPLE SAY THAT SPIES HANG OUT AT BOEING SURPLUS TO STUDY THE LEFTOVER PARTS AND EXTRAPOLATE FROM THEM HOW THE SYSTEMS FIT TOGETHER. THIS IS A GOOD WAY FOR ARCHITECTS TO LEARN THINGS, TOO, EXTRAPOLATING FORWARD INSTEAD, INTO NEW POSSIBILITIES.**

CHILDREN ALWAYS FIND IT MORE INTERESTING TO TAKE SOMETHING AND USE IT FOR [00230] **SOMETHING UNINTENDED. IT'S MUCH MORE FUN TO HOLD A TELESCOPE BACKWARDS AND SEND CLOSE THINGS FURTHER AWAY. COMPUTERS ARE LIKE THIS TOO. THEY'RE VERY GOOD AT TAKING JUMBLED INFORMATION AND PUTTING IT IN ORDER. BUT WE FIND THEM MUCH MORE INTERESTING FOR DISMANTLING ALREADY CONSTRUCTED INFORMATION INTO UNEXPECTED SURPRISES. EXPLORERS USED TO FIGHT THEIR WAY UP RIVERS LOOKING FOR HEADWATERS AND THE SINGULAR ORIGIN OF THINGS, THE SOURCE. INVENTORS AND ARCHITECTS HAVE ALWAYS WANTED TO MAKE UP PURE NEW SYSTEMS. NOWADAYS THOUGH, SYSTEMS ARE SO COMPLEX AND OVERLAPPING THAT THE REAL FRONTIER MAY BE DOWN ON THE DELTA, IN THE WELCOMING MUD AND FORKING STREAMS OF IMPURE NATURE AND INDUSTRY, LOOKING AT THE CONNECTIONS AND POSSIBILITIES, AND IMAGINING WHAT A CREATIVE OUTSIDER MIGHT FORGE OUT OF SOME OF THE SYSTEMS WE ALREADY HAVE.**

PACIFIC AVENUE

The Tideflats are set up best for big projects and relatively expensive solutions. [00240] Much of the time budget constraints force us to work with a little more ingenuity in the smaller shops of Pacific Avenue. Pacific Avenue is like any other strip in every other town west of the Mississippi, jumbling endlessly, full of excitement and opportunity. Alongside the gun shops is every imaginable business enterprise. Although we are most interested in the used car lots, we work primarily with [05500] small welding fabricators and autobody paint shops. To find creative people—the ones who can help figure out how to make new things from the wrong parts inexpensively—we go to where they're working on custom cars, or just keeping [05500] unlikely old cars running. Nobody knows odd shapes, bent pipes, or strange paint like a body shop. [09990] Most of the people working in these small shops were laid off from the shipyards when the industry moved to Asia, or they were welders on the nuclear plant at Satsop before that project shut down, or they worked on bridges and dams when these heroic things were still being built. There's no shortage of people who know how to do things.

Pacific Avenue, Tacoma's main street, runs north to south, a couple of very steep blocks uphill away from the Tideflats. Starting out downtown and paralleling the shoreline, it leads straight from the old city hall, past the banks and the Union Pacific terminal, past the light industrial yards and military bases, and eventually down, with a few twists and turns, to the foot of Mount Rainier. About halfway out there, Pacific Avenue changes its name to The Mountain Highway. Not far from where the name changes there's an elementary school where we first started our education. Probably because of the school, there was a traffic light across the highway at this point. The traffic light was important, because of the noise [11130] it created. There was a constant flow of log [01600] trucks coming down from the mountains, headed to the lumber mills on the Tideflats. At that time the trees were often still so big that there would be only one tree on each truck, cut into three log sections to fit on the trailer. If the light changed to red, the fast, heavily loaded trucks, three or four at a time, engaged their jake brakes, decelerating with a blatting roar in front of our classrooms. I learned a lot about jake brakes later from our excavator, Mac Fields, when I rode in his dump truck. Jake is short for Jacobson Engine Brakes. The brakes close the valves in the truck's [15400] engine to create a tremendous back pressure slowing down the drive train. It saves wear and tear on the wheel drums. They make a great noise. Nowadays they are illegal in cities.

ANOTHER GREAT SOUND ON FOGGY DAYS WAS THE PASSING WHEELS AND WHISTLES OF THE TRAINS BELOW OUR HOUSE. TO GET TO THE TRACKS WE WOULD SLIDE DOWN ONE STEEP HILL THROUGH TUNNELS UNDER THE BLACKBERRY BUSHES AND THEN CAREFULLY WORK OUR WAY DOWN A STEEP, CLAY CLIFF TO THE BEACH DOWN BELOW. THERE WERE TWO PARALLEL TRACKS BUILT—WITH GROSS RATIONALITY— DIRECTLY ON THE BEACH WITH A RUGGED ROADBED OF IMMENSE ROCKS TO PROTECT THEM FROM THE WAVES. THESE BEAUTIFULLY CONSTRUCTED TRACKS CARRIED PEOPLE AND COMMERCE [14910] FROM THE TIDEFLATS TO LOS ANGELES.

FOR SOME REASON, TRAINS HEADING SOUTH ALWAYS MAKE YOU THINK ABOUT LOS ANGELES. AND PASSING LOG SHIPS HEADING NORTH WITH THE SUN SETTING BEHIND THE OLYMPIC MOUNTAINS TRIGGER THOUGHTS OF THE PACIFIC OCEAN AND JAPAN. STANDING ON THE TRACKS YOU CAN FEEL A TRAIN COMING A LONG TIME BEFORE IT ARRIVES. PRESSING BACK AGAINST THE CLIFF YOU CAN ADMIRE THE PASSING FLATCARS, FILLED WITH TARPAULIN-WRAPPED LUMPS OF UNIDENTIFIABLE MACHINERY, HOPPER CARS WITH SAWDUST OR SAND, FORKED CARS WITH GIANT CEDAR LOGS, TANKERS, BOXCARS, AND SOMETIMES EVEN SPECIAL CARS WITH THE NOSE CONES, TAIL SECTIONS, OR FUSELAGES OF BOEING JETLINERS.

You couldn't miss the flow of trees. Walking home from school, there'd be chunks of bark and broken sprigs of fir branches all across the road. This stuff left sticky sap all over our fingers when we picked it up. Tree sap doesn't wash off. Children and carpenters know that the only way to get rid of the stickiness is to rub it down with dirt. The flow of trees out of the mountains was an enormous pres- [02070] ence. You could hear it, you could smell it, it stuck your fingers together.

Later we moved to a house with a high view of Puget Sound and the Olympic Mountain range. From there we saw a constant waterborne parade of log booms, mile-long corrals of fresh cut trees towed toward the tideflat lumber mills by tugboats. At night you could only hear the low thump of the tugboat's engine, but you could tell if there was a log boom by the number of lights on the mast and the eventual passing of a single weak light at the tail of the boom. On foggy [11130] days the engine thump carried more clearly, and they used their foghorns to navigate, timing the echoes off the invisible hills on the shore.

If the tugs weren't towing logs, then they usually towed a sand barge heading for a concrete plant. There was a sand and gravel pit on the shore a few miles south of our house. It was in the middle of a tall, wonderfully shaped hill covered with fir, cedar, and Madrona trees. They cut the hill out [02070] from the inside, making it like [02200] an artificial volcano. There were gates on the pit, but we knew what was going on because on Sundays, when we were in high school, we used to get into this crater and go off-roading with our old cars or pick-ups, dodging around the parked dump trucks, loaders, and rock crushers. A couple of years ago we discovered that the whole hill was gone and in its place was an ugly flat site filling up with more suburbs.

Pacific Avenue also leads out toward the big military bases. The other reason we could never hear much in school (besides the log trucks) was noise from the C-130 Starlifters. They roared off from McChord Air Force base and flew a few hundred feet over our heads. That was a horrible sound, but we liked to chase the giant shadows of the planes across the playground. We've made several projects out of those airplane shadows. At that time we didn't understand what we know now about the flow of trees or crushed rock or fill dirt. But the airplanes we understood even then. Lots of the kids had fathers in Vietnam. Tacoma is surrounded by military bases. There are airplanes, soldiers, nuclear subs, shipyards, and Boeing plants. Even with this amazing constellation of vibrant enterprise, Tacoma always has a slightly on-edge melancholy related to far away places.

People in Seattle usually think of Tacoma as an ugly, bad-smelling, sprawling little military-industrial city. Who could argue with that? If we had grown up in Seattle maybe you could call us Northwest architects. In Seattle there exists a kind of pure image of the Northwest, and people who want to make good buildings sometimes think about a regional architecture of beautiful timbers and finely drawn construction joints. But the Northwest is bigger and a lot more interesting than that. In Tacoma people are more connected to the international zeitgeist: the Port of Tacoma; log ships for Yokohama; scrap steel for Pusan; moth-balled nuclear plants; rainforests in the Amazon; Saigon; Los Angeles; Vladivostock. If you keep your eyes open it's not that hard to figure out where everything comes from and where everything's going, but there are still lots of surprises in the world.

THERE WAS VERY LITTLE BEACH LEFT NEXT TO THE TRACKS, BUT GREAT STUFF WASHED UP ON THE LOWER BOULDERS OF THE RAIL BED. THE BEST STUFF WAS THE KELP, WHICH IS NOT NEARLY AS COMMON AS IT USED TO BE, BUT WHICH IS ONE OF THE GREATEST MATERIALS WE HAVE EVER GRABBED HOLD OF. THIS STRUCTURAL SEAWEED IS THE RICH, TRANSLUCENT, ROOT BEER-COLORED BULL KELP, CONSISTING OF A HEAVY, BULB-SHAPED HEAD THE SIZE OF A LARGE FIST WITH AN ELEGANTLY TAPERED 20-FOOT TAIL. THE LUMINOUS SKIN IS SMOOTH AND SLIPPERY. THE SLICK, TAPERED TAIL IS HARD TO GET A GRIP ON, BUT IF YOU GET A GOOD PURCHASE YOU CAN STAND IN THE MIDDLE OF THE TRACKS AND WHIP IT AROUND IN A 40-FOOT DIAMETER ORBIT, INCREASING IN VELOCITY UNTIL THE KELP BEGINS TO HUM AN AMAZING, HIGH-PITCHED HUM. EVENTUALLY IT WHIPS OFF INTO SPACE FAR OUT INTO THE WATER, OR MAYBE INTO THE FACE OF WHOEVER ELSE IS ON THE TRACKS WITH YOU.

BEFORE YOU SEND THE KELP INTO ORBIT THOUGH, YOU CAN CUT OFF THE TIP OF THE HEAD AND THE TAIL AND PLAY IT LIKE A SKINNY TRUMPET, OR YOU CAN POP SOME OF THE AIR-FILLED BLADDER SACS ATTACHED TO THE RUBBERY SHEETS OF PLUMAGE GROWING OUT OF THE BULB. YOU CAN EVEN TRY TO BREAK INTO THE INNER SPACE OF THE BULB ITSELF AND TRY TO FIGURE OUT WHAT THIS SLIPPERY, TUBEROUS CAVERN AND ITS INTERIOR PLUMBING ARE ALL ABOUT.

1

AFFORDABLE PREFABRICATION

ANDERSON ANDERSON

OLD GROWTH AND ENGINEERED WOOD

WE USED TO WORK WITH A LOT OF OLD GROWTH, HIGH-ELEVATION DOUGLAS FIR LUMBER. THIS WAS NOT UNUSUAL IN THE NORTHWEST, WHERE EVERYONE HAD BIG FIR TREES IN THEIR BACKYARDS AND UNTIL MORE RECENTLY THE FORESTS STRETCHED AS FAR AS THE EYE COULD SEE IN EVERY DIRECTION UP AND DOWN THE MOUNTAINS. DOUGLAS FIR FROM THE FORESTS OF OREGON, WASHINGTON, AND BRITISH COLUMBIA IS GENERALLY REGARDED AS THE WORLD'S BEST FRAMING LUMBER; MANY OF US ALSO REGARD IT AS THE WORLD'S MOST BEAUTIFUL FINISH LUMBER FOR FINE WOODWORK AND FURNITURE. SLOW GROWING, OLD-GROWTH TREES FROM VIRGIN FORESTS MANY HUNDREDS OF YEARS OLD, WITH TRUNKS SOMETIMES 12 FEET IN DIAMETER AND MORE, PRODUCE A FINE, DENSE WOOD. TREES FROM HIGH IN THE MOUNTAINS WHERE THE SUMMER GROWING SEASON IS VERY SHORT—AND HENCE THE SOFTER, PULPY, SUMMERTIME RINGS OF GROWTH ARE VERY NARROW, AND THE HARD, WINTERTIME RINGS DOMINATE—HAVE PARTICULARLY TIGHT, BEAUTIFUL GRAIN.

UNTIL RELATIVELY RECENTLY THERE WAS STILL PLENTY OF OLD-GROWTH AVAILABLE, AND WE WOULD FRAME THIS BEAUTIFUL, HARD, HEAVY WOOD INTO THE HIDDEN INTERIOR WALLS OF HOUSES BY THE TRUCKLOAD. OFTEN WE WOULD COME ACROSS PIECES OF FINISH GRADE LUMBER AMONG THE FRAMING LOADS, AND IF TIME ALLOWED WE SAVED THIS FOR INTERIOR PROJECTS. OF COURSE, USING THIS OLD-GROWTH FIR HAS BEEN A LARGELY UNNECESSARY CRIME AGAINST THE COMPLEX ECOSYSTEMS OF THE NORTHWEST FORESTS. WE SHOULD HAVE KNOWN BETTER EARLIER, BUT WE HAVE SINCE CONCENTRATED A LOT OF THOUGHT AND EFFORT ON WORKING WITH ALTERNATIVE, LESS DESTRUCTIVE WOOD PRODUCTS, ESPECIALLY ENGINEERED WOODS AND BUILDING ELEMENTS THAT RELY ON RECONSTITUTED WOOD FIBER AND OTHER FAIRLY RECENT HIGH-TECHNOLOGY PRODUCTS. NOT ONLY HAVE THESE ENGINEERED WOOD PRODUCTS OFFERED NEW OPPORTUNITIES FOR ENVIRONMENTALLY RESPONSIBLE CONSTRUCTION, THEY ALSO HAVE ENGINEERED A SUBSTANTIAL LEAP IN THE STANDARDIZATION AND SOPHISTICATION OF WOOD FRAMING SYSTEMS. THE WOOD PRODUCTS INDUSTRY USED TO BE EXTREMELY OLD-FASHIONED, BUT IT IS NOW AMONG THE MOST INNOVATIVE INDUSTRIES IN TECHNICAL RESEARCH AND NEW-PRODUCT DEVELOPMENT.

TECHNOLOGY AND 2X4S

Architects are always fascinated by the idea of mass-produced housing that is both affordable and provides nice living for everybody. This has been one of the energizing aims of modern architecture. Strong social and political ambitions underpin these projects, as well as a strong technical interest. The world has received some great modern housing projects, some incredible ideas, many noble failures, but few enduring, truly rationalized systems. The biggest disappointments seem to come when only one of these two interests—social planning or technology—is present in a project. Recently there have been pleasant, banal, cheaply built houses arranged in progressively described, comfortably old-fashioned, socially streamlined community patterns. For the most part, it is difficult to argue with the pleasantness. It is easier to argue with the politics, the architecture, and the newly unreal urbanism. Our experiments with technical rationalization have not concentrated on the development of substantially new systems but instead have concentrated on increasing the flexibility of current systems to best accommodate the site-specific requirements of existing environments and urban conditions.

STRIPES

MANY BUILDING PRODUCTS SUCH AS SIDING AND ROOFING COME IN REPETITIVE MODULES, AND WE ARE OFTEN INTERESTED IN EMPHASIZING THE NATURE OF THIS FIELD AND ITS PATTERNS. IN SOME PROJECTS WE USE ALTERNATING MODULES TO EMPHASIZE AN IMPORTANT SUB-GEOMETRY, LIKE THE FALL-LINE (GRAVITY WATER COURSE) OF A SLOPING LANDSCAPE OR A ROOF THAT OTHERWISE CONFORMS TO ANOTHER PRIMARY GEOMETRY, AS IN THE TONN AND ENLOW HOUSES. IN THE ENLOW HOUSE WE BECAME INTERESTED IN THE ABILITY OF THE ALTERNATING SIDING PANELS—WHICH VARY IN WIDTH ACCORDING TO THE SPECIFIC ORIENTATION OF EACH SLICE OF THE WALL IN RELATION TO THE OVERALL, MOUNTAIN FALL-LINE GEOMETRY OF THE SITE AND THE ROOF—TO GEOMETRICALLY BREAK UP THE MASS OF THE BUILDING AGAINST THE GRAY ROCK AND GREEN VEGETATION OF THE CLIFF. IN THE TONN HOUSE WE HAD SIMILAR INTERESTS ALONG WITH THE THOUGHT OF DISSOLVING THE LARGE MASS OF THE SOLID WALLS OF THE HOUSE SO THAT WINDOWS AND WALLS MIGHT BOTH SHARE A KIND OF APPARENT TRANSPARENCY, OR AT LEAST AN UNCERTAIN DEPTH AND PLANARITY.

IN A LARGER MODULAR PROJECT LIKE THE HOTA PROTOTYPE APARTMENTS, THE STRIPES AGAIN EMPHASIZE THE CONTINUOUS FIELD OF THE WALL PLANE RATHER THAN THE MODULAR REPETITION OF THE HOUSING UNITS, WHILE OFFERING A VISUAL DISSOLUTION OF THE HEAVY MASS OF THE BUILDING WITHIN THE FINER-GRAIN COMMUNITY OF MOSTLY SMALLER BUILDINGS. THEY ALSO SERVE TO INTEGRATE THE VEGETATION ARMATURES AND THEIR PLANTINGS INTO THE MASS OF THE BUILDING ITSELF.

Most of the technical approaches invented by architects and engineers concentrate single-mindedly on the elegant redesign of the pieces of the project that are not problematic. Most technology-driven affordable housing initiatives have dealt primarily with the development of new, rationalized, modularized, factory-produced framing systems. As creative and seductive as many of these systems can be, even a superbly engineered system will be more expensive and less flexible than the one that we already have in 2x4 Western platform framing. Before we began working in Japan and started to understand the evolved rationality and organization of the American wood framing systems, we had not realized this. As we taught Japanese contractors how to build with 2x4s, we started describing this standard way of building an American wood house as a highly developed, fine-grained modular system.

Most architects think of standard 2x4 framing as the lowest, dumbest, and most cobbled-together of all building methods. Because it is cheap to build and easy to detail, this is a major type of construction for most single-family houses, a lot of multi-family housing, and many commercial projects. Unfortunately, it is also increasingly used in inappropriate ways—such as very large, synthetic-stucco-clad urban apartment and condominium projects. These poorly designed and poorly built structures will quickly deteriorate, undoing much of the recent progress in many cities towards increasing the density of urban housing. Although that is another story, it needs to be clear that we are not talking about that stuff when we talk about 2x4's. There are wrong ways and right ways to do everything. We are concentrating on subtle improvements to the ways that are generally right.

One of the main reasons that 2x4 construction is easy for architects to detail is the same reason that it is cheap: everybody in America already knows how the system goes together (or thinks they do). Because the carpenters and the contractors know how to put the system together, it isn't really necessary to instruct them in any great detail, so architects don't really have to understand that much about how it works themselves (or think they don't). This is changing in some areas, as building codes change to require greater resistance to earthquakes and windstorms, but such [01060] requirements introduce another big problem in architects' separation from the building process: the increasing over-reliance on the expertise of engineers. Shifting substantial design issues to other fields removes a large area of essential architectural creativity.

Two-by-four construction, properly understood as a remarkably well-developed, fine-grained modular [13120] system fully integrated across a sophisticated industry of sub-disciplines and parts manufacturers, is a field of opportunity wide open to creative tweaking. It is this framework of standards, shared knowl- [01091] edge, and networked distribution that serves as the starting point for much of our more recent work.

MASS PRODUCTION AND SITE SPECIFICITY

When we work on a project we are not primarily interested in the object of the building itself, or in the objects and connections of its parts. The interests that typically guide us—the development of the interior space and the experience of the space in relation to its surrounding context—become problematic when it comes to thinking about how to make pre-fabricated housing. Designing affordable mass-produced housing is necessarily focused on the production of the parts, the assembly of the [01043] parts, and the administration of the construction process. The site and its occupants are perceived of necessity as abstract variables rather than as specific generators of form and space. In this process, [13120] modular housing systems usually reduce the assumed context and house dweller to some lowest common denominator, the assumed-to-be-most-typical site and customer. In any realistically considered urban or natural context, few sites are flat and without significant environmental issues. Certainly our experience in the Northwest and in Japan, particularly with sites that are affordable rather than ideal from the point of view of easy construction access, [00230] is that no site begins as a flat, lowest-common-denominator site, and few home dwellers fit the inflexibly pre-determined expectations of typical lifestyles. The primary objective in any standardized building system should be the potential to individualize and adapt to the challenges and opportunities of unique situations.

STRIPES AND NAILS

But the stripes of the Kennedy project have another lineage as well—this is a house of a different stripe. Ever since one of our first roofing jobs, we [07520] have wanted to build a house sided with stripes of asphalt roll-roofing. On a hot roof, doing a dull, tedious job, your mind sometimes drifts to thoughts of vandalism. On that project we had the perfect excuse for mischief because there were two colors of roofing present and nobody had told us which of the many rolls of roofing—a whole load of leftovers from other jobs—we were supposed to use, or even that the house should be only one color. With stripes we could at worst be half wrong, while with either solid color we had a 50 percent chance of being completely wrong. Ever since then we have thought that stripes are an honorable mark of indecision—and indecision, or at least a decision maximally postponed, has always been our most fiercely preserved operating method.

[06050] The other reason we were in a surly mood that morning was the nailing method required. At best roofing nails are a painful experience: their tips are very sharp in order to pierce easily through the roofing material, the shaft of the nail is short because roofing is relatively thin, and the heads are unusually large to prevent them from piercing through the thin roofing material too easily. Most nails—which are not so sharp anyway—have a small head and a width-to-length ratio that allows them to lie in an organized side-by-side fashion in your nail bags so that you can scoop out a handful and use them in a painless fashion. But roofing nails get jumbled in your nail bags, and you can't pick up a handful without getting stabbed.

The house in question had an open-beamed ceiling, and we were nailing directly into the structural decking—which was also the finish surface of the ceiling below. If this system is used correctly, there are many layers and many inches between the nailing surface of the roofing and the finish surface of the ceiling. In this case, there was exactly a half-inch of plywood, exposed as the ceiling below. All the parts of the roof were slimmed down with such penny-pinching creativity as to be essentially unworkable. Of the many associated problems with this roofing system, the one that concerned us most was the consequent maximum length of the wicked little roofing nails. The shaft of the nail was so short there was no room to squeeze your fingers between the head of the nail and the razor-sharp mineral granules on the surface of the asphalt. There was just room to prop the nail against your little finger to hold it upright in preparation for a blow of the hammer. You could either then bring the hammer crashing down with great speed and accuracy, pulling your finger out at the last fraction of a second and driving the nail home just before it toppled over; or else employ a more conservative two-stroke approach, in which you would lightly tap the nail head in the hopes of gaining sufficient, minimal purchase in the roofing so that it could stand on its own until the second, harder stroke of the hammer set it home.

Once a routine was established, the first method was the least painful, because then you could pull your fingers away without scratching them on the asphalt. But occasionally the heavy hammer would catch your finger just before it pulled out and smash it flat between the nail head and the scathing granules. The second approach was safer overall, but involved unavoidable, nail by nail, bloody abrasion of the skin. There are more nails per square foot in roll roofing than in any other roofing system. By the end of the first row, when the striping decision needed to be made, we were definitely in the mood for a retaliatory prank. God and the devil are in the details.

KENNEDY HOUSE

FOX ISLAND, WASHINGTON 1993

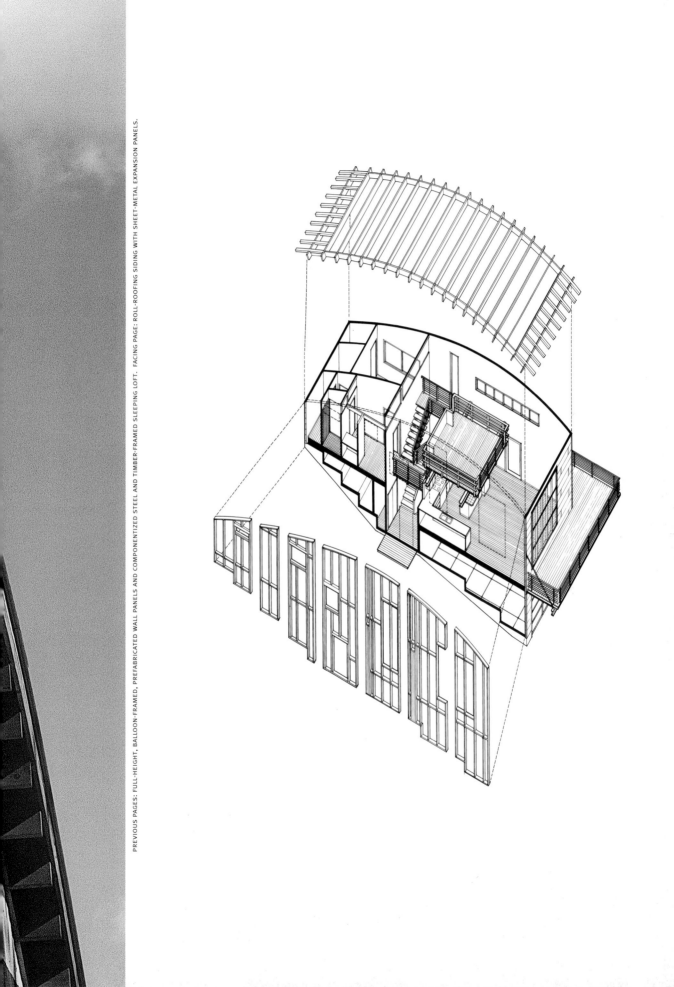

DEVELOPMENT COSTS

In Japan—as in larger development projects in the United States—affordable housing sites are often developed as massive land-engineering projects that reduce complex natural and urban environments to flat, easily buildable sites. The costs of this approach to land development are enormous—ecologically, aesthetically, and financially. For many reasons—land ownership patterns and population density among them—land prices in Japan are already very high, and these civil engineering costs are considered insignificant in the overall cost of the land. Construction costs are highly compartmentalized in calculating housing prices in Japan. The end of the business that we are primarily engaged in—the last phase, physical construction of the house object—is frequently approached as an internal financial calculation outside the larger context of land development costs and general business and public infrastructure overhead. This compartmentalized approach to the big picture, though highly organized, has effects on the landscape that are sometimes as destructive as the disorganized, free-market development of land in the United States.

In America, the total project costs are more fully evident in the financial analysis of a project, but we have other problems that contribute to a simplistic inflexibility in affordable housing design. Land is cheap and bulldozers are cheap, so we also—in cheaper, sloppier ways—make any house fit any site, torturing the land and the eventual occupants into an uncomfortable relationship to a building system that is rational only at the grossest scale. This pattern is followed not only in affordable, pre-fabricated projects, but also for the most part in expensive custom house projects individually crafted on site. There are many reasons for this, but basically it all boils down to the fact that design, forethought, and an architect's passionate pursuit of ideas are too often regarded as slow, expensive, vaguely unsettling, and largely unnecessary.

BALLOON FRAMING

For a number of years we have been working on a series of houses, apartment buildings, and small commercial buildings in the U.S. and Japan that are constructed as simple boxes of balloon framing, proportioned to accommodate standard-dimension lumber framing spans in transportable panels. To maximize the strength of the panels for transport, to create maximum flexibility in window layout, and to expose the richness of this standard structure, the framing is continuous through most window openings. The windows are inexpensive, standard

08000
aluminum units joined together on site with square aluminum tubing and placed outside the 2x6 wall framing that continues uninterrupted through the window openings. This method eliminates the need for trimmers and headers, thereby 01050 reducing cost and weight and allowing easy flexibility in window size and placement without altering the panel layouts. The elimination of headers is important, because these are frequently larger-dimension timbers from larger trees.

STRIPES AND MANAGEMENT

BY THE TIME WE BUILT THE KENNEDY HOUSE, OUR COMPANY HAD GROWN TO THE POINT THAT WE HAD STARTED TO EXPERIMENT WITH RATIONALIZED CONSTRUCTION MANAGE- 01043 **MENT SYSTEMS. WE HIRED A NUMBER OF PROFESSIONAL, WELL-QUALIFIED CONSTRUC-TION MANAGERS WITH EXPERIENCE IN VERY LARGE, HIGHLY ORGANIZED INTERNATIONAL CONSTRUCTION COMPANIES. WE HAD BIG PLANS. PROFESSIONAL CONSTRUCTION MAN-AGERS, HOWEVER, ARE TRAINED TO ANTICIPATE AND AVOID PROBLEMS, NOT SOLVE THEM. THIS MAY APPEAR TO BE A GREAT IDEA, BUT IT INVOLVES A HUGE AMOUNT OF PAPERWORK, SECOND-HAND RESEARCH, AND THE STRICT AVOIDANCE OF EMPIRICAL EXPERIMENTS. WE BECAME TOTALLY APPALLED TO DISCOVER THAT WE WERE PAYING PEOPLE TO AVOID LIABILITY BY ASKING OTHER PEOPLE WHO WERE PAID TO AVOID LIA-BILITY HOW NOT TO BUILD THINGS IN THE WAYS THAT WE WERE PAYING OTHER PEOPLE TO DRAW THEM. WE HAD INADVERTENTLY SET INTO MOTION MANY FRUSTRATING AND EXPENSIVE MANAGEMENT LOOPS WITHIN OUR COMPANY—TO THE EXTENT THAT OUR OWN MANAGEMENT SYSTEM CONSPIRED TO DENY US OUR STRIPES. ONE CONSTRUC-TION MANAGER'S CALL TO A ROOFING MANUFACTURER'S TECHNICAL REP HAD CON-** 07520 **FIRMED THAT USING ASPHALT ROLL ROOFING ON A VERTICAL SURFACE WOULD VOID THE WARRANTY. AFTER THAT, THE BATTLE WAS ON INSIDE OUR COMPANY.**

01091
THE TECHNICAL REPS SAID THAT THE COEFFICIENTS OF EXPANSION WERE SUCH THAT ROLL ROOFING WOULD SLUMP AND SAG ON A HOT DAY IF IT WERE USED ON A VERTICAL SURFACE. THIS WAS BEFORE SLUMP AND SAG BECAME VERY POSITIVE CONCEPTS AT THE CORE OF OUR DESIGN THINKING, AND THIS DIDN'T SOUND GOOD EVEN TO US AT THAT POINT. ON THE OTHER HAND, WE HAD SEEN ROLL ROOFING USED ON THE SIDES OF BARNS BEFORE—WE THOUGHT, OR AT LEAST SAID THAT WE HAD—AND THEREFORE WE ARGUED THAT AT LEAST IN A PLACE LIKE WESTERN WASHINGTON WHERE IT NEVER GETS REALLY HOT, THIS MATERIAL SHOULD WORK JUST FINE AS SIDING. AT THE SAME TIME, WE HEDGED OUR BETS, WHICH ALSO ADDED TO THE VISUAL INTEREST OF THE PROJECT. WE REDUCED THE SLUMPABLE AREA OF THE MATERIAL BY CUTTING EACH 36-INCH WIDE ROLL IN HALF AND APPLYING IT IN NARROWER STRIPES. WE ALSO USED A MAXIMUM OF TEN-FOOT LENGTHS, INSERTING A SMALL SHINGLE OF GALVANIZED SHEET METAL 05800 **BETWEEN EACH PANEL AS AN EXPANSION JOINT. THE LOCATION OF THESE SHINY EXPANSION JOINTS VARIED, BECAUSE EACH ROLL HAD ONE SHORT LENGTH LEFT AFTER THE TEN-FOOT SEGMENTS WERE CUT, AND EACH LEFT-OVER WAS USED AGAIN AT ITS CONSEQUENT LENGTH, GIVING A SYNCOPATED BUT ENTIRELY RATIONAL AND ECONOMICAL VARIEGATION TO THE FIELD. THE OWNER AND HER FAMILY DID ALL THE NAILING—WE GAVE THEM LONGER NAILS THAN WE HAD BEEN GIVEN IN OUR FIRST EXPERIENCE WITH THE MATERIAL, BUT WE DIDN'T REALLY WARN THEM OF** 00240 **EVERYTHING WE KNEW. WITH THE FREE LABOR AND CHEAP MATERIAL, THE WHOLE SID-ING JOB COST HER ONLY A COUPLE HUNDRED BUCKS. IT DIDN'T SLUMP (VERY MUCH).**

The 2x6 wall framing exposed at these openings establishes the fin- 06200 ish system for the entire structure. Finish materials and surfaces are created from inexpensive framing-grade lumber and from quick, framing-style carpentry methods for easy completion by homeowners or less skilled labor. The exteriors of the buildings are clad in a variety of inexpensive materials, including galvanized steel and granulated asphalt products, as well as various types of wood and cement-based siding panels.

Although inexpensive to construct, the buildings are designed to offer rich spatial experiences. In several of these projects, the arching wood ceilings, visible from many points in the interiors, continue uninter- rupted from room to room to allow the eye a view of a ceiling plane curving out of sight beyond each 08000 room's glass-panel-topped dividers. The stairs and bedroom lofts float suspended in space, allowing mul- tiple views and filtered light throughout open interiors—provid- ing a sense of spatial limitlessness as well as of mystery and privacy. The building elements are reduced to simple, practical pieces chosen to provide a meaningful presence in the occupants' experience. The bookcase-lined bedroom lofts float 13010 like rafts in the air beneath the warm arch of a wooden sky. The hanging decks expose an explicitly straining structure of tension and compression to reinforce a sense of hanging out on the face of the building, just as the suspended, open staircases built of 2x4s in 06170 a scissors-like cantilever reinforce the lightness and separation of the floating rafts above.

The open and efficient interior spaces give the feeling and livability of larger rooms, allowing the inhabitants to live happily in smaller and more economical structures. We have chosen the materials for their low energy requirements during manufac- turing and processing, and also for their low long-term maintenance requirements and ability to be recycled. The adaptability of the structures for a variety of site conditions eliminates the need for destructive, homogenizing site leveling, and allows for optimizing sunlight and view exposure, saving existing vegetation, and adapting to local street and urban conditions.

At the time of the Kennedy and Hota prototype projects, engineered wood products were still relatively
06170
expensive, less than common in America, and not yet approved by most building codes in Japan. These projects were very basic experiments in using traditional 2x4 wood members and framing techniques.
06100
To be affordable, and to minimize the environmental impact of inappropriate wood use, these projects were designed with short structural spans and light loads. The relatively small-dimension wood members required could be cut in standard lengths from small, fast-growing trees from replanted, sustainable-yield forests.

The short spans of these lumber products contributed greatly to the shapes of these buildings and their interior spaces. We derived the width of the Kennedy house from the maximum span of standard length rafters. The curve of the roof is made as inexpensively as possible, without any custom truss or beam elements, by simply curving the top of the
06100
wall and laying standard joists along the curve, no differently than if it were a flat floor or roof. The curve is actually cheaper in this case than any other way to make this roof. It would have required more carpentry, more wood, more complex roofing systems, and more interior volume to create a standard pitched roof form. Even a completely flat roof would have been costlier, because we would have needed a much more expensive, flat-roof waterproofing system. In this case the roofing is inexpensive corrugated steel. The radius of the roof curve is the maximum amount of curve that would allow us to force bend—with the weight of several carpenters—the straight roofing panels down to the curve without the expense of having the panels machine-rolled to the curve at a factory, or facing the shipping inefficiencies of curved members. Shipping rules and
06100
container dimensions are a key influence on all the construction elements. There are many layers to the origin of particular formal and spatial possibilities, and to the affordability of achieving them.
00240

FULL HEIGHT PANEL ADAPTED TO
SLOPING SITE CONDITION.

TRANSPARENT DOCUMENTATION

At the same time that we have been working on the physical components of pre-fabrication, we have also been investigating the systematization of design and construction management, pre-fabricating these administrative procedures within computer applications. Although most of this work involves relatively dry management documents streamlining the construction process, we have also become quite fascinated by linking drawing and administrative programs to rapidly adapt large subsystems to specific site conditions.

Working with multiple layers of transparency generated in modeling software, our drawings have begun to merge assembly systems into three-dimensional models that allow the simultaneous analysis of many building components in relation to one another. This kind of multi-dimensional, multi-layered transparency offers tremendous opportunity for a comprehensive understanding of the buildings' bones, skin, and organs, and all of the connections between them. This process, and the resultant drawings and models, have had a strong influence on our spatial thinking. Trains in the City, for example, involves a transparent specifications document, which is designed for simultaneous readings and a comprehensive understanding of all layers and dimensions of the project. Many of our ideas about space, documentation, and creative project management have come directly from practical analysis of construction problems in these prefabrication projects.

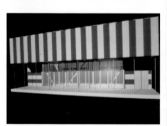

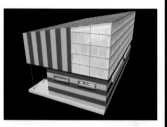

THIS PAGE: ZEBRA OFFICE PROTOTYPE, WASHIZU, JAPAN 1998. FACING PAGE: HOTA PROTOTYPE APARTMENT BUILDING, CHIBA PREFECTURE, JAPAN 1997.

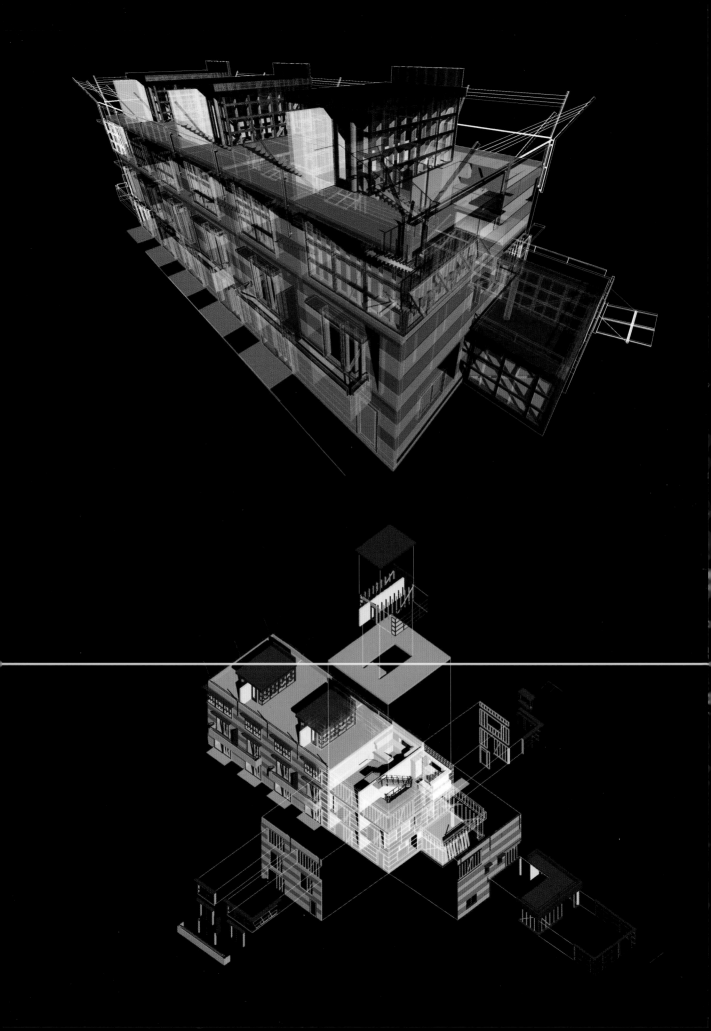

ECONOMICS, GLU-LAMS, AND SOCIAL CHANGE

2

HOMES AND SOCIETY

THE CHANGING ECONOMY OF CONTEMPORARY JAPAN HAS LED TO S GNIFICANT CHANGES IN THE WAY PEOPLE LIVE. TRADITIONAL HOME STYLES AND CONSTRUCTION SYSTEMS ARE NO LONGER APPLI-CABLE OR AFFORDABLE FOR MUCH OF THE POPULATION. NEW OPTIONS HAVE BECOME NECESSARY. DENSELY PACKED MULTI-FAMILY APARTMENT BUILDINGS HAVE ABSORBED MUCH OF THE URBAN INFLUX, BUT WITH RISING AFFLUENCE MORE FAMILIES HAVE SOUGHT HOUSING THAT OFFERS BETTER QUALITY OF LIFE AND MORE FLEXIBLE LIVING PATTERNS. DEMAND FOR SINGLE-FAMILY WOOD HOMES HAS BEEN HIGH EVEN ON EXPENSIVE URBAN LAND. WHILE THIS REQUIRES OWNERS TO GREATLY ALTER THEIR EXPECTATIONS OF BUILDING SIZE, MATERIALS, AND FORMS, THERE REMAINS AN ENDURING INTEREST IN INCORPORATING TRADITIONAL ENTRY, BATHING, AND SLEEPING AREAS. IT IS A PARTICULAR CHALLENGE FOR JAPANESE BUILDERS TO ACCOMMODATE THE TRADITION OF MULTI-GENERATION HOUSEHOLDS AT A TIME WHEN FAMILY STRUCTURE AND OBLIGATIONS ARE CHANGING, THE AVERAGE POPULATION AGE IS RAPIDLY INCREASING, AND IN-HOUSE CARE FOR ELDERLY RELA-TIVES IS NO LONGER A CERTAINTY.

ANDERSON ANDERSON

PREVIOUS PAGES: SHINOHARA PROTOTYPE, TSU-
RUGA, JAPAN 1994. THIS PAGE: AMERIKAYA
AFFORDABLE PREFABRICATED HOME PROTOTYPE
1, TSURUGA, JAPAN 1994.

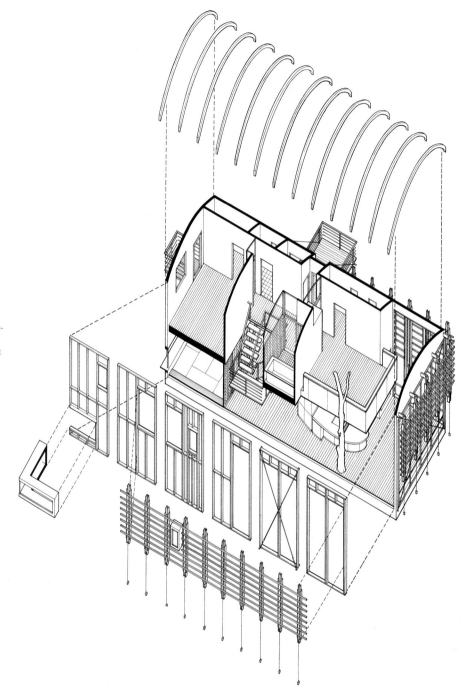

ACCESSIBLE MULTI-GENERATION HOUSING

We have had the opportunity to work with several Japanese construction companies which have sought to differentiate their offerings through innovative approaches to rapidly changing social conditions. We find these companies to be the most interesting project partners, as they allow us to combine our backgrounds in client- and site-specific design solutions with ideas for standardi-zation and systematization of affordable building 13120 systems. The Hota prototype was designed to use the cost efficiency and design flexibility of our panelized framing approach to produce a mixed-use urban apartment building accommodating the varying needs of differing family structures. The ground floor accessible housing units and retail space provide opportunities for the elderly and disabled to live independently, but in close prox-imity to neighbors, children, and grandchildren. The upper levels of loft-like townhouses with roof-top terraces provide a spaciousness to accommo-date a variety of family organizations.

A further development of these ideas as applied to the detached home market has come through our work with a Tokyo-based company that has also targeted the multi-generation housing mar-ket, where there is a desire to combine traditional extended family relationships with contemporary desires for increased privacy and independence. We developed a series of modular home proto-types that combine accessibility features, addressing the needs of the elderly and disabled, with multiple generation household zoning to allow the extended family to comfortably share the land and structure. Planning for adaptability and flexibility over time, the system consists of panelized base modules to which additional living spaces can be attached as needs change. The base plans are designed for tight urban building parcels, with expansion elements offered to adapt to irregular geometries and the exact dimensions of specific sites.

FINANCE AND GOVERNMENT

Affordable housing in Japan is generally financed by the Government Housing Loan Corporation, 00240 which—like the Federal Housing Administration in the United States—imposes additional regula-tions on construction standards and systems 01060 beyond the basic building codes. The specific rules of this agency, coupled with already strict import restrictions, zoning regulations, fire and

COURTYARDS AND GARDENS

ONE OF THE PRIMARY ATTRACTIONS OF SINGLE-FAMILY HOMES IS THE ABILITY TO DEVELOP ADDI-TIONAL PRIVACY IN BOTH INTERIOR AND EXTERIOR LIVING SPACES. ACHIEVING THESE GOALS ON THE SMALL INFILL SITES FOUND IN JAPANESE CITIES IS VERY DIFFICULT, AND FEW EXAMPLES OF CONTEM-PORARY MASS-MARKET HOUSING PROVIDE SUC-CESSFUL SOLUTIONS. SINGLE-FAMILY WOOD HOMES ARE THE TRADITIONAL NORM IN JAPANESE CITIES, BUT LAND COSTS ARE EXTREMELY HIGH. MOST NEW HOUSES ENTIRELY FILL THEIR SITES TO WITHIN ONE METER OF THEIR PROPERTY LINES, WITH NO LIVING AREAS OR OTHER TRANSITION SPACE BETWEEN THE INTERIOR AND EXTERIOR. THIS APPROACH IS DISTANT FROM THE JAPANESE TRADITION OF CREATING SEQUENTIAL LAYERS OF INTERIOR AND EXTERIOR SPACE.

PLANNING HOMES FOR SMALL URBAN SITES MUST FOLLOW THE SAME PRINCIPLES OF ALL GOOD DESIGN, INCORPORATING AWARENESS OF SUN, 00230 WIND, TOPOGRAPHY, VEGETATION, AND ALL OF THE CONTEXTUAL INFLUENCES OF A VIBRANT CITYSCAPE. EVEN WHEN THE ACTUAL SITE IS NOT YET KNOWN, AS WHEN WE ARE WORKING ON PRO-TOTYPE DESIGNS, WE MAKE ACCOMMODATIONS FOR THESE FACTORS BY ALLOWING FOR THE SELEC-TION OF ADAPTABLE MODULARIZED COMPONENTS. FINDING WAYS TO DEVELOP FLEXIBLE DESIGN SOLUTIONS FOR TYPICAL EXISTING URBAN SITES IN JAPAN HELPS MAKE IT POSSIBLE TO AVOID THE INCREASING INFLUENCE OF AMERICAN-STYLE SUB-05800 URBAN DEVELOPMENT PATTERNS.

THE SYSTEMS OF MODULAR HOUSING WE HAVE DESIGNED IN JAPAN INCLUDE USEFUL EXTERIOR SPACES AS ESSENTIAL PARTS OF THE PROGRAM, PROVIDING COURTYARDS AND PROTECTED TER-RACE AREAS—EXTENSIONS OF THE LIVING SPACES AND OPPORTUNITIES TO INTRODUCE NATURAL 13600 LIGHT AND VIEWS TO THE INTERIOR ROOMS WITH-OUT COMPROMISING PRIVACY. WHEN WE HAVE ALSO HAD THE OPPORTUNITY TO BE INVOLVED IN THE LAND DEVELOPMENT AND PLANNING, WE HAVE COORDINATED BUILDING PLACEMENT AND 02900 LAND PARCEL CONFIGURATIONS TO CREATE A SERIES OF OUTDOOR SPACES BETWEEN AND WITHIN THE BUILDINGS.

building codes, and a system of tax incentives related to affordable housing and social initiatives, all contribute to a complex regulatory context shaping the design of imported housing projects in Japan.

During the 1990s the import housing and construction materials business was a central focus of trade and economic policy discussion within Japan, and between Japan and the United States. Due to the large trade imbalance between these two countries, intense pressure was placed on those industries where there was a genuine Japanese domestic market for American goods and services. Alongside internal social and political changes in Japan affecting consumer expectations, an unprecedented period of rapid technological advances in American wood products (in part related to depletion of forest resources and increasing pressure of environmental politics in the United States), macro-economic policies bumping against the traditional practices and code restrictions of two very different countries produced a continually shifting and bewilderingly complex construction environment affecting what might otherwise be thought of as simple house building. It has been exhilarating and immensely educational to be swept from the particularities of a Seattle job site into close confrontation with the rippling consequences of large international systems in motion.

We were invited to participate in the Chiyo New Town project, a development of affordable housing co-sponsored by the Japanese Ministry of Construction and the city of Kitakyushu. Designated a "lead project" in import housing initiatives by the national government, the project was conceived as a demonstration of new construction systems and a research project in lowering Japan's typically high building costs. Our role was not as architects in this project. Our company provided a team of superintendents and staff to lead building crews from five Japanese construction companies. All of the issues of construction systems, building codes, and trade policy converged in this project. Because governments and large companies were involved on all sides, and much of the purpose of the project was to examine the effects of policies, codes, and regulations on the design and building process, many issues ordinarily taken for granted were brought up for discussion and negotiation. The actual progress of change is very slow, of course, but once the systems are revealed and called into question, and seemingly little issues are linked to big issues, many possibilities can be considered. This project has had a great deal of influence on much of our subsequent design work, setting particular ideas into the context of larger systems, and the possibility of shifts within them.

MODULAR MANAGEMENT

The use of pre-designed modules has been a fundamental strategy for many of our projects in Japan. By standardizing and repeating certain pieces, such as particular roofing sections, kitchen modules, or a two-level stack of bathing and toilet areas, we have simplified the process of designing and ordering materials for the more complicated sections of buildings. Materials lists, design details, and building plans for these modules are then combined with a reduced number of custom elements to adapt the buildings to their sites. Although most of the projects have been designed around wall panels that can be prefabricated at a remote location and brought to the site in building containers, the true modules in these cases are not just physical sections, but design and administrative modules streamlining the construction management process. Whether the buildings end up being panelized or stick-built on site, the greatest part of the cost efficiency comes from savings in design time, construction management, and reduction in errors and waste related to materials ordering. Particularly in Japan, but also in the U.S., these portions of the project budget are far more important than the framing costs alone, as we have learned from working through many comparative cost studies, and

through the costly and not infrequent jobsite disaster of too many people standing around waiting for one worker to drive to a local hardware store to pick up a
crucial 59-cent box of staples forgotten in the million-dollar load of construction
materials shipped to the site.

CONSTRUCTION LABOR AND PREFABRICATION

Much of the innovation in the competitive Japanese construction industry, following the model of the automotive industry, focuses on mechanizing and automating
the building process. Several large manufacturers have produced proprietary
modular framing systems, some of them using elegant, patented connectors and
mass-produced parts. Many of the systems generate entirely steel-frame buildings, which assemble like highly sophisticated scaffolding systems. We have studied these systems carefully and have been involved in several research projects
sponsored by both the U.S. and Japanese governments comparing them to
American-style wood framing—which never seems to be beat in terms of cost efficiency, design flexibility, and performance as part of an integrated structural and
building envelope system. The biggest advantage of the standardized wood framing is the "open system" nature, which involves many competing suppliers of
equivalent parts and a high level of openness to innovation and integration with
other systems when needed.

One of the biggest problems faced by the wood home building industry in Japan
has been the shortage of skilled carpenters, as fewer and fewer new apprentices
enter the profession. Out of this need factories both in Japan and the U.S. have
made a number of attempts at pre-panelized home systems, building wall sections
in the largest segments transportable and ready for assembly on site. We have
had the chance to work with these systems in a number of different ways and have
established our own approaches to integrating panelized building elements into
our projects. The greatest shortcomings we have found in most panelized systems
currently available has been the limitations on design flexibility, and the narrow
focus on wall sections only—a high level of site labor is required for flooring and
roof systems. We also have found that the cost and availability of carpentry labor
are highly variable in the different regions of Japan and different seasons of the
year, making it difficult to predict the actual cost savings of off-site panelization.
Another factor that tends to diminish the viability of prefabricated systems are the
extremely high inland transportation costs in Japan, where it can often cost more
to transfer materials ten miles from port to jobsite than it does to get them from
the American lumber mill to the Japanese port.

Working through these issues on several projects, we have found that a hybrid of
systems and materials provides better and more flexible solutions than any one
system used by itself. Although it requires exceptions to the basic Japanese building code, which discourages a mixing of structural systems within a single project,
we have had particular success with introducing a system of prefabricated steel
seismic frame elements which greatly expand the design flexibility of wood structures. As the Japanese building code often exempts carports from building setback
restrictions, we have used these steel seismic frames as carport structures to span
from the house to the lot line, gaining required parking spaces underneath upper
floor rooms without the intrusion of structural columns, while at the same time
opening up window and door opening flexibility in other parts of the building.

FOLLOWING PAGES: CHIYO NEW TOWN PROJECT, KITAKYUSHU,
JAPAN 1995. AFFORDABLE HOUSING EXPERIMENT UNDER
DIRECTION OF JAPAN MINISTRY OF CONSTRUCTION AND
KITAKYUSHU HOUSING DEPARTMENT.

3 HYBRID FRAMING

WINDOWS AND STRUCTURE

THERE ARE FEW ISSUES IN THE MAKING OF A HOUSE THAT DON'T REVOLVE AROUND THE WINDOWS. SUNLIGHT, AIR, VIEWS, AND PRIVACY SHAPE THE WINDOWS. TO A LARGE EXTENT, THE WINDOWS SHAPE EVERYTHING ELSE. THE RELATIONSHIP OF THE WINDOWS TO THE STRUCTURAL INTEGRITY OF THE BUILDING FRAME IS ESPECIALLY IMPORTANT. IN WOOD STRUCTURES, WINDOWS ARE A PAR-
TICULARLY VEXING PROBLEM. MAKING WOOD BUILDINGS ON VIEW SITES, WE DEVOTE A MAJOR PORTION OF THE DESIGN AND ENGINEERING TIME TO STUDYING THE WINDOWS IN RELATION TO THE STRUCTURAL SYSTEM.

WHEN PROPERLY BUILT, WOOD BUILDINGS ARE EXTREMELY STRONG AND RESISTANT TO HEAVY WINDS AND EARTHQUAKES. THE DYNAMIC STRENGTH AND FLEXIBILITY OF THEIR FRAMES ALLOW THEM
TO ABSORB HEAVY FORCES. JAPAN INCREASED ITS INTEREST IN WOOD-FRAME BUILDINGS AFTER THE DEVASTATING KOBE EARTHQUAKE, WHEN HOUSES BUILT WITH 2x4 FRAMING FARED BETTER THAN
MOST OTHER STRUCTURAL SYSTEMS IN USE. THE STRENGTH OF THIS WOOD BUILDING SYSTEM RELIES ON LARGE EXPANSES OF PLYWOOD-COVERED WALLS RATHER THAN ON THE RIGID FRAME CON-
NECTIONS FOUND IN STEEL AND CONCRETE CONSTRUCTION. FOR THIS REASON IT IS ALWAYS A BATTLE TO ACHIEVE LARGE EXPANSES OF GLASS WHILE AT THE SAME TIME MAINTAINING A STRONG BUILD-
ING. WE ARE CONSTANTLY TRYING TO FIGURE OUT AFFORDABLE WAYS TO CREATE THESE BIG WINDOW AREAS—IT WOULD BE SIMPLE, OF COURSE, IF THERE WERE NO BUDGET LIMITATIONS INVOLVED.
THIS IS THE MAIN REASON THAT SO MANY OF OUR BUILDINGS ARE HYBRIDS OF SEVERAL FRAMING SYSTEMS RATHER THAN ONE PURE SYSTEM. WE USE AS MUCH OF EACH SYSTEM AS IS PRACTICAL
AND EFFECTIVE IN ACHIEVING THE MULTIPLE GOALS OF THE PROJECT. IN ADDITION TO STANDARD 2x4 WOOD PLATFORM FRAMING, WE INTRODUCE OTHER STRUCTURAL ELEMENTS—STEEL, CONCRETE,
STRESS-SKIN SANDWICH PANELS, GLU-LAM POST AND BEAM—TO ACCOMPLISH SPECIFIC GOALS, VERY OFTEN RELATED TO ISSUES OF THE WINDOWS OR THE CREATION OF LARGE, UNINTERRUPTED
ENVELOPES OF SPACE.

THERE ARE THREE PRIMARY WAYS TO ACHIEVE LARGE WINDOW AREAS. ONE IS TO BUILD LONG WALLS WITH WINDOWS IN THE MIDDLE AND SIGNIFICANT AREAS OF SOLID SHEAR PANEL AT THE ENDS,
OR WITH SHEAR PANELS INTERSPERSED WITH THE WINDOWS. THIS IS THE BASIC SYSTEM. FOR MORE GLASS AREA WITHOUT SOLID SHEAR PANELS IN PLANE WITH THE WINDOW, ONE CAN BUILD REL-
ATIVELY SMALL DIMENSION STRUCTURAL STEEL FRAMES WITH RIGID JOINTS THAT RESIST BENDING UNDER SIDEWAYS FORCES. THESE ARE SOMETIMES EXPENSIVE, BUT WE USE THIS APPROACH IN
SPECIAL SITUATIONS AND USUALLY EXPOSE IT AS A SIGNIFICANT PART OF THE IDEA OF THE BUILDING. THE THIRD METHOD INVOLVES TRANSFERRING FORCES FROM ONE AREA OF THE BUILDING TO
SOLID, SHEAR-RESISTING ELEMENTS IN OTHER AREAS OF THE BUILDING. THIS REQUIRES CONSTRUCTING VERY RIGID FLOOR OR ROOF DIAPHRAGMS, OFTEN USING STRESS-SKIN PANELS, WHICH WILL
CARRY FORCES FROM THE OPEN GLASS WALL TO INTERIOR SHEAR WALLS OR OTHER SOLID WALL AREAS. THIS IS THE ESSENCE OF THE SYSTEM WE USED IN THE MARONTATE AND ESS HOUSES, AND
THE STRUCTURALLY EFFICIENT CURVED FORMS OF THESE HOUSES WERE LARGELY THE RESULT OF THE INTERRELATED AMBITIONS OF THE WINDOW WALLS WORKING IN HARMONY WITH THE RESOLU-
TION OF THE FORCES THEY GENERATE.

MARONTATE RESIDENCE

PREVIOUS PAGES: PREFABRICATED
GLU-LAM STRUCTURE WITH STRESS-
SKIN SANDWICH PANEL DECKING.

The Marontate house can only be explained in relationship to the light, views, and topography of its site. At the same time, the primary focus of the project is the relationship of these site conditions to the structural systems chosen to accommodate them.

The site is a steep, south-facing hillside, with panoramic views overlooking Puget Sound, the city of Tacoma, and Mount Rainier. To either side neighboring houses look directly across the site, diminishing privacy and intruding on the dramatic 180-degree views. To open the house with an uninterrupted glass wall, while maintaining the clients' privacy, we worked from the earliest sketches on a semi-circular form wrapping around a large private deck. A solid wall on the outside north-facing curve and a glass wall on the inside curve facing south over the cliff create privacy for the house and deck. Structurally, this half-doughnut shape transfers all lateral loads through the roof to the solid outer shear wall, enabling the inner wall's uninterrupted stretch of glass. The curved form also acts as a highly efficient dam-like earth retaining wall, creating the uphill entry courtyard area—the only flat terrace on an otherwise extremely steep site.

We were able to achieve the large sweeps of open interior space and window wall only by fully exploiting the capabilities of the hybrid glu-lam, stress-skin sandwich panel and steel column framing system. The offset radii of two intersecting arcs, which form the structure and enclosure of the building, give the house its crescent shape. This offset is born of the sun shading issues as well as the practical requirements of the plan, which required a large space in the center for the main living area and smaller spaces at either end of the circle for a bedroom and a music room. While the plan was best accommodated with a crescent shape, the roof structure was far more economical as a simple, semi-circular structure of equal bays. Thus, the rational structural arc of the roof structure, which is supported on thin steel columns and an arcing glu-lam beam, is separated from and pierces through the non-structural arc of the window wall. All the horizontal wind and seismic shear forces acting on the view side of the building are then transferred through a stress-skin sandwich panel roofing system to the solid back wall facing the street.

The differential arcs of the roof and the enclosing wall below are also situated for optimal sun shading. The two arcs are most nearly tangent at due south where the incoming sunlight is at its most vertical. The arcs diverge, creating deep overhangs towards the ends of the crescent, which offers greater shading for more horizontal sunlight in morning and evening. The lower angles of the sun in the winter bring light deep into the house through much of the day.

A service wing extending back into the hillside ties the building structurally and visually to the site. The main crescent shape is thus able to remain one continuous open space, subdivided and defined only by freestanding sculptural/functional elements such as the kitchen, the bedroom closet, and the stone fireplace. At the intersection of the main crescent and the service wing stands a four-story tower, housing the main entry and twin studies that capture spectacular marine and mountain views. A metal-clad bay window at the top of the tower is cocked toward Mount Rainier, offering a specially framed view from John Marontate's desk. Viewed from the outside, the window suggests an animate nod of the house toward its site.

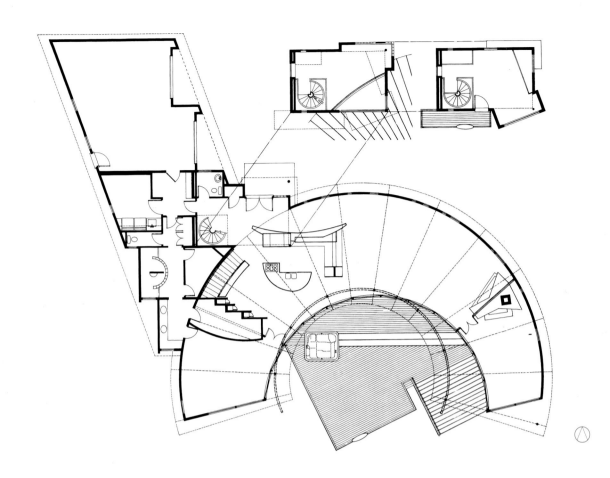

FRAMING IN THE AIR

A LOT OF WHAT WE KNOW ABOUT FRAMING WE LEARNED FROM MARTY. WE
HAD ALREADY BEEN BUILDING FOR A NUMBER OF YEARS WHEN WE FINALLY
HAD ENOUGH BUSINESS, AND GOOD SENSE, TO HIRE A REAL CARPENTER.
BEFORE THAT WE HAD BUILT A LOT OF DECKS, COMPLICATED ADDITIONS,
AND WHOLE HOUSES, LEARNING THE TRADE ON OUR OWN, AND MOSTLY
HIRING ASSISTANTS WE COULD AFFORD. USUALLY THEY WERE GREAT PEO-
PLE, OFTEN WITH AMAZING STORIES TO TELL AND MUCH TO TEACH ABOUT
THE PARTS OF LIFE WE HADN'T RUN INTO YET, BUT NOT A LOT MORE TECH-
NICAL KNOWLEDGE ABOUT BUILDING THAN WE HAD. MARTIN MACDONALD
WAS OUR YOUNGEST EMPLOYEE AT THIS POINT, NOT MUCH OLDER THAN
EITHER OF US, BUT HE'D BEEN WORKING IN CONSTRUCTION SINCE HIGH
SCHOOL, HADN'T SPENT TIME IN ARCHITECTURE SCHOOL, AND HAD A
WEALTH OF BUILDING KNOWLEDGE BECAUSE OF IT. MARTY HAD NEVER
BEEN A LEAD FRAMER AT THAT POINT. HE WAS FAST AND EFFECTIVE, BUT
TOLD US HE DIDN'T HAVE THE EXPERIENCE TO LAY OUT COMPLICATED
PROJECTS LIKE RAFTERS AND STAIRS. WE THOUGHT THIS WAS NO PROB-
LEM, AS WE'D BEEN DOING ALL OF THAT OURSELVES FOR YEARS. WE BUILT
A COUPLE MORE HOUSES TOGETHER, AND IT DIDN'T TAKE MARTY LONG TO
REALIZE THAT ALTHOUGH HE WAS STILL INEXPERIENCED COMPARED TO HIS
PREVIOUS BOSS, HE KNEW A LOT MORE THAN WE DID. IT'S THE OPPOSITE
OF WHAT YOU MIGHT EXPECT: ALTHOUGH TRAINED AS ARCHITECTS, WE
HAD NEVER REALLY APPROACHED BUILDING PROJECTS METHODICALLY AND
SYSTEMATICALLY. WE STARTED OUT BUILDING EVERYTHING BY TRIAL AND
ERROR. THIS WORKED WELL ENOUGH FOR A WHILE, PROVIDING OPPORTU-
NITY FOR CREATIVE CONSIDERATION AND CHANGE THROUGHOUT THE
PROCESS. BUT IT WAS A SLOW WAY OF DOING THINGS, AND IT KEPT US
FROM DEALING WITH THE BIGGER PICTURE. MARTY, ON THE OTHER HAND,
KNEW FRAMING AS A SYSTEM. THERE WERE METHODS AND SEQUENCES,
MATHEMATICAL PROCEDURES, GEOMETRY, AND SPATIAL LOGIC.

WE HAVE NOW HAD THE CHANCE TO WORK WITH MANY EXCELLENT
FRAMERS. IN THE HIERARCHY OF CONSTRUCTION TRADES, FRAMERS ARE
VASTLY UNDERRATED. FINISH CARPENTERS ARE MORE HIGHLY REGARDED
CRAFTSPEOPLE. WOOD FRAMING IS OFFICIALLY REFERRED TO IN THE
CONSTRUCTION SPECIFICATIONS INDEX BY THE TITLE OF ROUGH
CARPENTRY, AND FRAMERS ARE OFTEN THOUGHT TO BE LESS SKILLED AND
ROUGHER. IN REALITY, GOOD FRAMERS MUST HAVE REMARKABLE SKILLS
IN PROJECTING AND UNDERSTANDING THREE-DIMENSIONAL SPATIAL RELA-
TIONSHIPS. FROM ABSTRACT DIAGRAMS THEY WEAVE COMPLEX CON-
STRUCTIONS. THIS PROCESS IS NOT ENTIRELY STEP-BY-STEP. MUCH OF
THE FINAL INTERRELATIONSHIP OF STRUCTURAL MEMBERS AND SPACE
MUST BE WHOLLY UNDERSTOOD, MULLED OVER, DEBATED, AND STRATEGI-
CALLY PLANNED FROM THE VERY BEGINNING. FINISH CARPENTERS, ON THE
OTHER HAND, LITERALLY HAVE A FRAMEWORK TO BUILD THEIR WORK
AROUND. THE SPACE AND LIMITS OF THEIR WORK ARE FULLY DEFINED BY
THE FRAMER. GOOD FRAMERS TAKE INTO THEIR CALCULATIONS EVERY
SUBSEQUENT STEP IN THE CONSTRUCTION PROCESS, TO FACILITATE THE
WORK OF EVERYONE WHO FOLLOWS: PLUMBERS, MECHANICAL CONTRAC-
TORS, DRYWALLERS, ROOFERS, AND FINISH CARPENTERS. THEY ALSO
MUST BEGIN THEIR OWN PHASE BY CORRECTING ERRORS LEFT BY THE
ARCHITECTS OR THE FOUNDATION CREW.

ANDERSON ANDERSON

ISHIDA FERRARI GALLERY

TOKYO, JAPAN 1996

In addition to prefabricated production housing in Japan, we have had the opportunity to design a number of larger, more site-specific projects, always using hybrids of American and Japanese building systems. The Ishida Ferrari Gallery houses a display space for a collection of classic Ferrari automobiles. It also contains associated warehouse storage spaces, as well as a residence for the family of the gallery owner. For the area—a busy, low-rise neighborhood of residential and retail buildings—this is a relatively large structure located on a relatively small corner lot. The building is organized around a central courtyard. The residential and warehouse areas form the rear "L" of the courtyard, and the gallery area forms the forward "L" of the courtyard, facing onto the adjacent streets. The two-story living spaces open onto the courtyard, with large expanses of glass facing to the south and east. The lower gallery wings buffer the living areas from the street but allow the south and east light to pass over into the courtyard and the living spaces beyond and below. A glass greenhouse structure above a portion of the gallery brings sunlight into the main display areas as well as enabling sunlight to pass through onto the courtyard. This lightweight glass structure above the otherwise private, blank-walled building provides a subtle, emblematic image for the automobile gallery below. The owner's study, configured like the pilot's position in a fighter jet or in a Ferrari, is an efficient round cockpit suspended above the main gallery space.

INTERIOR OF GALLERY SPACE VIEWED FROM COCKPIT STUDY.

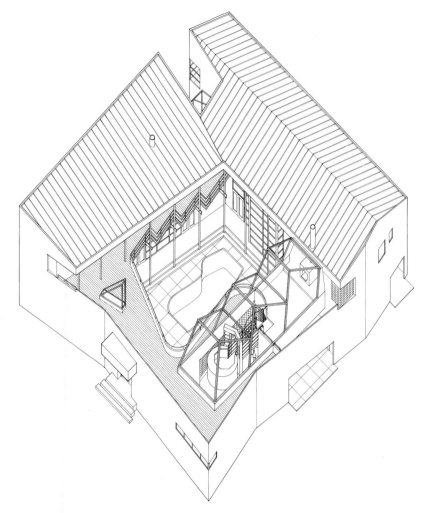

AXONOMETRIC VIEW FROM SOUTHEAST

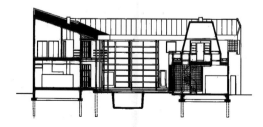

WEST-EAST SECTION

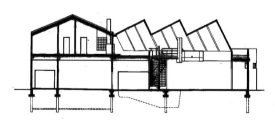

NORTH-SOUTH SECTION

SCHOEPP/THORNTON BLOCK HOUSE

FORT WORTH, TEXAS 1996

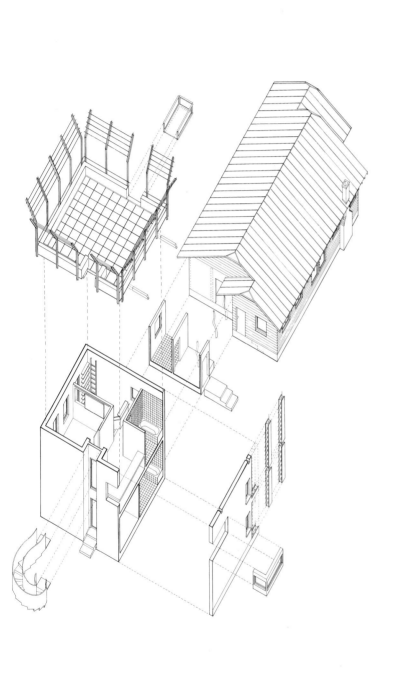

We have spent a lot of time in Texas working on projects with sculptor Cameron Schoepp. For the past ten years Cameron has been gradually rebuilding the small wooden house he lives in with his family. We all worked together on figuring out how to expand the house without a major disruption to their living situation. Their initial thought was to add a second story onto the existing early 1900s bungalow, but we ended up pushing for a very different approach, partly because they intended to live in the house during the building process. We used to do a lot of addition and remodeling projects, working for months at a time in the eerie light beneath dripping, wind-whipped, blue plastic tarpaulins stretched tight across the ripped-open roofs of our building projects, with highly disrupted, highly worried clients living beneath our feet. There is no such thing as a quick, clean remodeling project once the roof goes away.

The other reason we rejected the idea of a second story addition was that we all liked the existing structure very much just the way it was. We felt it was extremely important to maintain the scale of the street by keeping the present house intact, building the new addition in the backyard. The neighborhood shared this pattern, with any number of odd outbuildings constructed in the backyards of the simple older homes.

There are several beautiful old pecan trees in the backyard, providing a deep pleasant shade on a hot summer day and an amazing network of shadows in the winter. The available building area within the circle of trees was limited to 20 square feet in order to avoid damage to the tree roots. To replace the outdoor space in the backyard lost to the new addition, we designed a rooftop sculpture court on the top of the two-story block, surrounded by a trellis for growing a wall of vines. Sitting amidst the singing birds in this sun-dappled space within the boughs of the pecan trees, looking over the rooftops toward distant views of the city, one completely escapes the immediate neighborhood.

The block of the house itself is simple and extremely dense. It grows directly out of ideas in Cameron's recent sculpture work, which frequently involves very raw cast materials—concrete, iron, lead—constructed as heavy and forbidding geometric solids enclosing only-hinted-at interior volumes of rich and mysterious complexity. The exterior of the building is constructed entirely of two simple materials—natural cement plaster on concrete and raw rusting steel. The interior has an only slightly richer palette, adding natural wood elements alongside cement plaster and steel.

The building structure uses a remarkable material of prefabricated lightweight concrete planks, erected in small modules, then reinforced and grouted in a manner similar to concrete block structures. The planks can be sawn like wood, and are therefore very flexible to use. Known as Rastra Block, the material was developed in Austria and more recently licensed for manufacture in Mexico, with this house being one of the earliest instances of its use in the United States. Its high insulation value coupled with a high thermal mass make it an ideal material in the extremes of hot and cold temperatures encountered in Texas. It is also more resistant to fire, bugs, and dry rot than the typical wood building.

In addition to the Rastra Block, there are a few cast concrete elements, such as the computer desk and slit window on the second floor, and a good deal of welded steel. Cameron's work—and much of the work we do together—involves a lot of casting and welding. The detailing of this house is developed entirely around these processes. There are no finishes on the materials used on the exterior of the house. The steel is allowed to rust and slowly bleed its trace into the natural cement surface of the stucco. We are all fascinated by this patterning of rust, which is highly developed in traditional Japanese construction and is also the source of so much beauty in post-industrial America. Woven with the slatted shadows of the pecan trees against the screen of the wall, the rust streaks dissolve the building—visually and literally—into its site.

4 PUBLIC IMAGINATION ——————————————

Machinery, materials, and business practice represent one important stream of influence on what gets built and how things get built. There are many other less tangible but equally powerful systems affecting architecture. The exchange of ideas and imagination within the field is central to the pursuit of significant architecture, but architects' ideas and the processes of implementation clearly take place within larger economic, social, and political systems.

Much of the creative work involved in design and building concentrates on the middle and end zones of the entire construction process, while relatively little creative attention is paid to the pre-schematic design phases where most of the limitations and ambitions for a project are firmly set. It is easy to say that much architecture, especially in America, is conceived and built with astonishingly little imagination, ambition, or even recognition of the opportunities missed. There always seems to be a great deal of corporate interest in restructuring the services of architects in the commissioning and administrative processes of design projects, but most often these discussions seem superficial, conservative, and narrowly focused on financial advantage rather than on the potential to dig into the guts of the whole process and reinvent the early phases of programming and schematic design.

We have been thinking about the role of public imagination in the creation of architecture. One side of this involves the awakening and harnessing of genuine creative thinking among the public about just what sort of world might be built. The other side involves the effective communication of ideas that architects wish to present for receptive public consideration. Many of our projects have evolved from an intended expansion of architectural possibilities by creatively integrating the disparate practical ambitions of various fields and points of view into compacted double- and triple-duty transformers that generate something more than the sum of their parts. We have been very excited about harnessing and provoking this kind of shared public imagination, and have been trying to figure out how to start productive discussions among a broader set of participants related to important public projects. The Evergreen Forest Canopy Study Center evolved through a number of public and semi-public cross-disciplinary events, which sought to generate creative participation beyond the architecture profession.

At the same time we began working on the Evergreen project we were involved in forming a new forum for the interdisciplinary discussion of art, architecture, and urban issues in Seattle. The first major project of the Space.City forum was a series of lectures and events intended to spur active public imagination in the design of Seattle's new central library. An important project in its own right, it also had the potential to expand into a broad discussion of urban culture in Seattle. We were asked to present one of these events, and we planned it as an open discussion addressing the possibilities and challenges for a new library in the dawning age of post-material, post-book information systems. To provoke discussion at a significant level of architectural creativity, we decided that we would stage a warm-up to the discussion with a rapid-fire conversation of short, provocative thoughts. We invited architect Andrew Zago and choreographer Crispin Spaeth to participate in generating a series of compacted idea fragments.

MA: Let's invent a public process to invent the new public library. I've
01200
seen on TV that public process consists of a very long table at the
02100
front of a room, where decision-makers and experts sit facing a large
room of the public. The experts present a plan. The public comments on
the experts' plan. This is not very imaginative and it doesn't harness the
initial creativity and energy of the public. The public is used primarily in
a critical role, not in a creative role. We need a process of creative public conversation. Spatial discussion rather than linear, bilateral discussion. New technology could facilitate this flowering of public
speech, and then also set it into a productive order.
00240
AZ: Rapid change in both technology and user expectations can be anticipated for the new Seattle
Library. Determine the estimated construction and maintenance cost of a new library over a rea-
sonable life expectancy for the facility and instead of building something, immediately distribute
that amount evenly over that time span as an annual construction budget.

08000
MA: Maybe the library will have no exterior presence in the city. There will be many doors
on many streets. Great, wonderful doors that speak of the public majesty of libraries and
learning. But nowhere, up and down the street, will there be the walls of a library. The
library will be corridors, caverns, and tubes hollowed out of the insides of every other
kind of building, and the reader will wander through these labyrinths, navigating by bea-
cons of light cascading down through incised worm-holes through the activities above,
discovering all kinds of great new possibilities, and never once leaving the library through
the same door entered. **CS**: Build a dissolving building, a honeycomb structure whose
ceilings and walls would gradually be removed as they become
unnecessary. Peel off roofs to create public gardens. As the sec-
02070
tions of roof get peeled off, transform other sections into
freestanding penthouse public housing units, and resident
motel units for scholars.

MA: The library will be clad entirely in flaps and
shutters opening into study booths, where particularly excited readers will occasionally jump
up, throw open the walls of their cubicle, and
shout their discoveries into the street. Citizens
08000
and tourists will stand on the sidewalk awaiting these outbursts of joyful or enraged learning as they marvel at the remarkable patterns
of human scholarship rippling across the walls
of the street—sometimes a simultaneous bab-
bling cacophony, sometimes a penetratingly singular exclamation on a blank white page.

INFORMATION. POLITICS. MATERIAL. BODY. A DISCUSSION OF LIBRARIES AND PUBLIC IMAGINATION

AZ: A book, as a thing, hovers between the projected space of reading and the sensate space
of the body. The book as a thing creates an arena for perception. The "thing" of books, of
data, of information should not be considered a by-product of reading or an obstacle to data
transmission, but as an intrinsic part of that form of knowledge. The Seattle Library should
base its handling, organization, and presentation of its books, electronic data, and other
information primarily on the quality of their presence and on their capacity to inspire. Only
second, if at all, should it consider issues related to the logic of classification, the ease of
handling, or the neutral uniformity of the material and spaces.

CS: Bring into the library experience good use of the physical
self to accomplish the task at hand. Clear thought can be mud-
dled by cultural assumptions about library behavior, and about
study in general. There are many possible manifestations of
emotional and muscular preparation for thought—putting on
thinking caps, furrowing one's brow in concentration, thinking
really hard, clearing one's mind for information to come in—all
manifestations which can inhibit clear thought.

MA: I just noticed in the mirror that the label was sticking up at the neck
of my sweater. Watching in the mirror, I reached up with my hand, but
could not find the back of my neck. I closed my eyes and fixed the label
right away. We rely too much on our vision to reconstruct mentally the
information that is already held as knowledge in our bodies. In a library
we will be working with our eyes and with our verbal intellects. The building that wraps itself around us should concentrate on the physical
knowledge and experience of our bodies. Our body-mind will read the
building, our verbal-mind will read its contents.

11130
CS: Interrupt the neutrality of the library. Include the experiential as well
as the referential. In the stacks, install walls of light, slowly changing
washes of luminous, solid color. This will enhance the drama of pursuit.

AZ: Create a system to commission original works. The library can sell all of its books and instead act
as a public agent to sponsor and publish new works. A list of potential writing projects is made available. For a modest sum, patrons can sign up to commission a particular project. When enough patrons
have signed on, the work is written, published, and made available to the general public.

MA: The library might be built of paper. Fine papers. Thick, crisp, translucent. Within thick covers. Blank, heavy, minimally identified in golden code, light bleeding through each leaf, becoming progressively darker as you proceed into the depths of paper. AZ: Create a mobile stack system—like trains in a train yard. Continuously alter the arrangement of stacks. Computer tracking and updated guides allow the same efficiency of search and storage as a fixed system. The new combinations of subject matter, however, create a surge in cross-disciplinary understanding and innovation.

CS: Assign a free wall for graffiti artists, a constantly changing exhibit of self-expression and a document of free speech.

MA: As children we floated in space and learned the world—eyes to a mirror walking down into the ceiling, floating into the train station dome, climbing and rolling in the distant balconies of the capitol. The world was space. We didn't know the Pantheon or St. Peter's. Imagination, experience and understanding occupied one seamless physical space. The world was not yet reduced to a cardboard language of signs. The world was still space. And we floated in it.

11130
CS: Have an outdoor soapbox, a platform with a microphone or bullhorn available for anyone who has something to say. With a time limit.

MA: Let's imagine all that we can imagine, but not be incapacitated with worry that we must anticipate every new possibility, becoming obsessed with flexible accommodation and empty anticipation of the future. This is another interruption of history. We empty our present in mock deference to the past or empty our present in quaking fear of inhibiting the future. The future will be smarter than we can be.

AZ: The library should not be light or translucent or fleeting. It should be the densest building in Seattle. As dense and terrible and luxuriant as the landscape.

MA: The new library should be a lead box with nothing inside. There is too much information floating around us. We are drowning in junk mail and TV and digital communication. There is no empty space now for the formulation and consideration of knowledge. We don't any longer need a building to store precious information. Information floats all around us. We have plenty at home. We need a silent room to think. A silent public room of many thinkers.

MARK ANDERSON, ANDREW ZAGO, AND CRISPIN SPAETH. SEATTLE ART MUSEUM. MAY 15, 1997

CS: Should we be talking about a public library and public transportation at the same time?

MA: Half of the library would be suspended in silence, half within the chaos of children, sunlight, and machines. The contrast would be physically overwhelming, each space wrapped in a thick and indefinable transitional emptiness. We would weave back and forth between the dark vacuums of comfort or terror and the physical salvation awaiting us in the noisy worlds of light. Threatening madness chases us back and forth between the library's twin lobes.

08000
MA: Imagine an intrusive, tentacular building of many doors, leading into a swelling, shrinking, rising, falling maze of corridors, book stacks, and reading rooms winding within buildings over and under streets, up and down hills—one long smelly library connecting cookbooks to restaurants, tree books to gardens, history books to dusty basements, poetry to coffee shops, politics to cigar shops, medicine to hospitals, fashion books to discotheques.

01091
AZ: Exchange branches with another library in a foreign city. Or merge the Seattle Library with another library in a foreign city of comparable size, but with a different focus and with a different set of expectations from the community it serves. Create a single database, ready access to each other's collections, continual video projections of each other's reading room and other civic spaces. Provide a travel budget for citizens to visit each other.

11130
AZ: A programmable information infrastructure can be incorporated into the building. Protruding objects, glowing wall panels, electronic billboard-style light surfaces, wind tunnels, and other environmental features can react to any desired data set. When using the library one is also inhabiting information. An economist, a sociologist, or a political activist can use the library to dynamically chart global trends as a visceral experience. Beyond this use, the building can be considered a giant instrument. Like a church organ, the library can be played by performing artists.

02100
MA: The new library is a controversy. I didn't know this until recently. What is controversial about a library? Is the passion about real estate, taxes, and political turf? Are we impassioned by the utter importance of such a sacred public space? Can we argue about all the wonderfully conflicting possibilities for what the library can mean, and the idea that will be imbedded in its construction, and the defining role it may play in the physical and intellectual future of the city? Can the discussion rise above a petty understanding of political confrontation to become a
01200
great public intellectual debate as creative and stimulating for this city as our highest dreams for the building itself?

This project was our first opportunity to frame and plumb a literally vegetable space of dynamic phenomena—the swaying treetops of a Northwest forest. The Evergreen State College is a public liberal arts institution with a progressive, highly interdisciplinary curriculum. The school's existing campus is a connected series of brutalist concrete structures set into the middle of a diverse forest preserve adjacent to the city of Olympia, capital of Washington State. The buildings are nicely designed, from a visual point of view, although none of our clients at the school seem to agree with us on that estimation. They feel that the closed concrete structures cut them off entirely from the forest they inhabit. This site is uniquely appropriate for a forest access structure, with its juxtaposition of the natural environment, education, and politics.

We think of this project as both a good example of what results from a process of public imagination and an armature for continuous activities of imagination in the future. Initially the scope of the project involved finding some place in the nearby woods to build a system of access to allow a broader spectrum of students and public to visit the remarkably rich and little-known world of life at the tops of trees. Environmental biologist Nalini Nadkarni, the client and creative co-collaborator on the project, led a series of public meetings bringing us together with diverse groups of scientists, artists, scholars, students, and community representatives to develop ideas for the structure. As a result we have synthesized a very open, flexible armature for diverse activities in the treetops. Rather than placing the structure apart from the campus buildings, we proposed to link it directly to the heart and brain of the school, its library, and at the same time to plumb into the school's steam plant, telecommunications, and essential utilities.

The building program, when looked at from the simplest level, involves the construction of an aerial hike through the forest canopy. This accessible walkway will take off from the third floor of the library and wind up through, around, and within the roots and boughs of the forest. The walk will be punctuated by a series of events and platforms for scientific experiments, instruction, and public viewing. A seminar room will be the major way station on the hike. This shuttered room will hover within the forest canopy like a ship floating in the rolling waves of the sea and provide a year-round, multi-purpose meeting and performance space in the treetops.

EVERGREEN STATE COLLEGE, OLYMPIA, WASHINGTON 1998

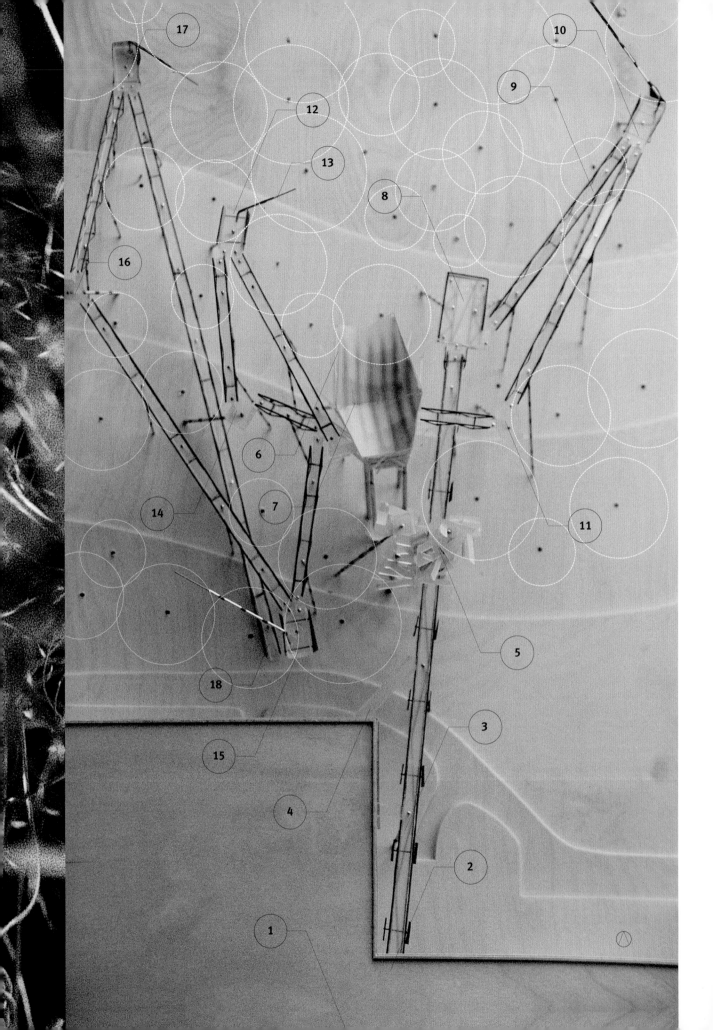

1 FOREST PULPIT: A LECTURE PLATFORM RUDELY ADDRESSING THE MAIN CAMPUS PLAZA; THE CANOPY TRAIL MARQUEE GUIDING VISITORS OUT OF THE CAMPUS, THROUGH THE LIBRARY LOBBY, AND OUT INTO THE FOREST. **2** BRIDGE PENETRATION INTO LIBRARY AND ADMINISTRATION BUILDING LOBBY. **3** THE CANOPY BRIDGE WILL BE A STEEL RAMP STRUCTURE SUPPORTED ON SLENDER STEEL STILTS AND PROVIDED WITH ALTERNATING TRELLIS SCREENS FOR GROWING FOREST EPIPHYTES. IT WILL BE A CONTINUOUS RAMP MEETING STATE UNIVERSAL ACCESS CRITERIA. THE WALKWAY WILL BE EQUIPPED WITH STEAM, IRRIGATION, AND MISTING HOSES CONNECTED TO THE SCHOOL'S NEARBY STEAM GENERATION FACILITY. THESE UTILITY HOSES WILL PULSE AND FLOW ALONG THE STRUCTURE FEEDING THE CREATION OF VARIOUS MICROCLIMATES AND EXPERIMENTAL ENVIRONMENTS. **4** GANG PLANK ACCESS TO LIBRARY VERANDA. **5** THE EPIPHYTE SCREEN WILL BE A VERTICAL, DISH-SHAPED SCREEN OVERFLOWING WITH PLANTS AND STEAM-HEATED MISTS. THE CANOPY TRAIL WILL PASS THROUGH THIS SCREEN, CREATING A SENSE OF PASSAGE INTO A MYSTERIOUS NEW WORLD. WITHIN THE BACK OF THIS VEGETATED SCREEN WILL BE A PROJECTION SCREEN. IN FRONT OF THIS SCREEN WILL BE A SMALL LECTURE AND PERFORMANCE STAGE. **6** THE CANOPY SHIP IS A GLASS, STEEL, AND WOOD SEMINAR ROOM STANDING HIGH IN THE TREETOPS. THERE WILL BE A SHUTTERED GLASS EXTERIOR ENCLOSURE AND A SHUTTERED PLYWOOD INTERIOR ENCLOSURE THAT CAN BE OPENED TO LIGHT AND AIR OR CLOSED FOR DARKNESS AND THE PROJECTION OF IMAGES. **7** THE MOSS BED THEATER WILL BE AN OPEN AIR, DISH-SHAPED SPACE ON TOP OF THE CANOPY SHIP. THE FLOOR OF THIS SPACE WILL BE A LARGE, HOT WATER-FILLED BLADDER. A DEEP LAYER OF SOFT MOSS WILL BE GROWN ON THIS STEAMING, IRRIGATED SURFACE TO PROVIDE A TREE-TOP MEADOW FOR VIEWING MIDNIGHT FILMS OR LISTENING TO AFTERNOON CONCERTS IN THE FILTERED LIGHT OF THE CANOPY. **8** FOREST ECOLOGY LECTURE DECK. **9** CANOPY TRAIL: FIRST LEG; ALUMINUM TRUSSES, WOOD DECKING, HYDRAULICALLY DAMPENED STILTS. **10** WESTERN RED CEDAR INTERPRETIVE DECK AND RESEARCH BOOM. **11** ALDER GROVE INTERPRETIVE DECK. **12** WESTERN HEMLOCK INTERPRETIVE DECK. **13** CANOPY ACCESS BOOM: HYDRAULIC EXTENDING CRANE FOR FLEXIBLE ACCESS TO RESEARCH PROJECTS. **14** ELDERBERRY INTERPRETIVE DECK. **15** DOUGLAS FIR INTERPRETIVE DECK AND RESEARCH BOOM. **16** WESTERN MAPLE INTERPRETIVE DECK. **17** UNDERSTORY INTERPRETIVE DECK AND RESEARCH BOOM. **18** CANOPY TRAIL LANDING; SYSTEM ELEVATION 0.

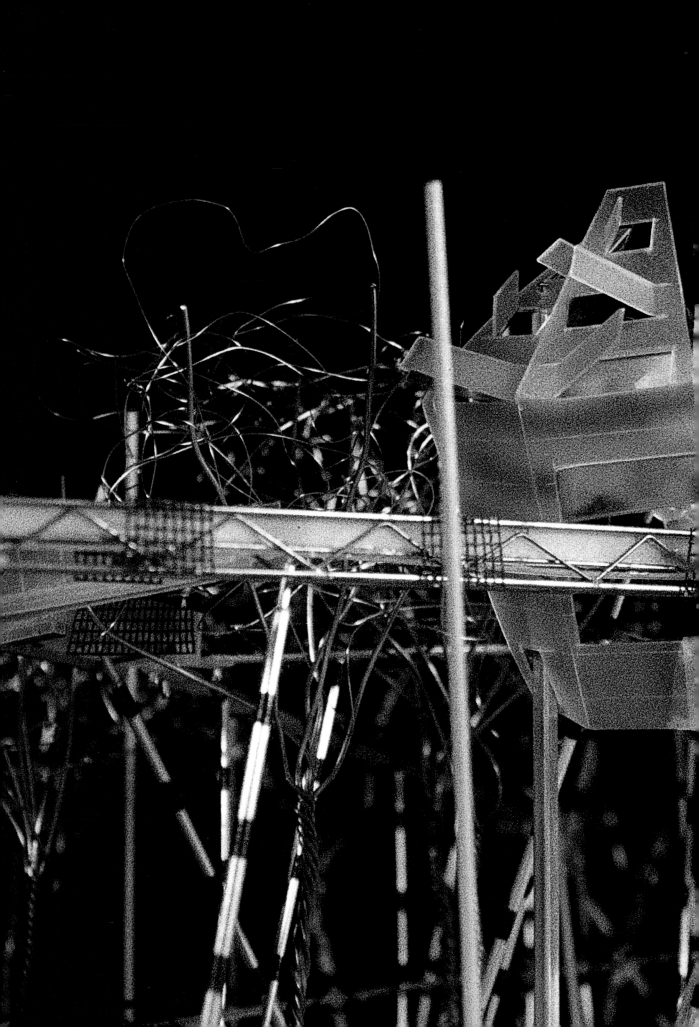

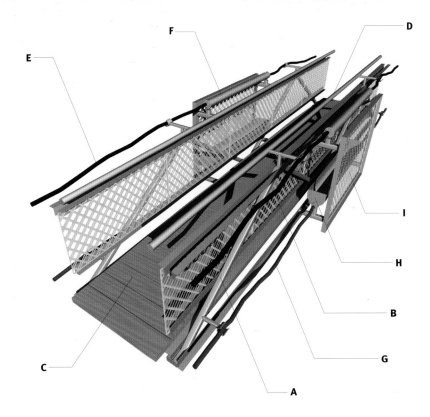

A WELDED ALUMINUM TRUSS STRUCTURE. **B** EXPANDED ALUMINUM GUARDRAIL. **C** 3x8 PRESSURE-TREATED DOUGLAS FIR DECKING. **D** ALUMINUM HANDRAIL. **E** STEAM SUPPLY LOOP WITH HIGH-PRESSURE RUBBER HOSING. **F** STEAM MISTING MANIFOLD. **G** COLD WATER SUPPLY LOOP. **H** HOT WATER SUPPLY LOOP. **I** PLANT RESEARCH SOIL CONTAINER WITH INTERIOR WATER SUPPLY MANIFOLD AND VALVE SYSTEM FOR MICRO-CLIMATE ENVIRONMENTAL CONTROL.

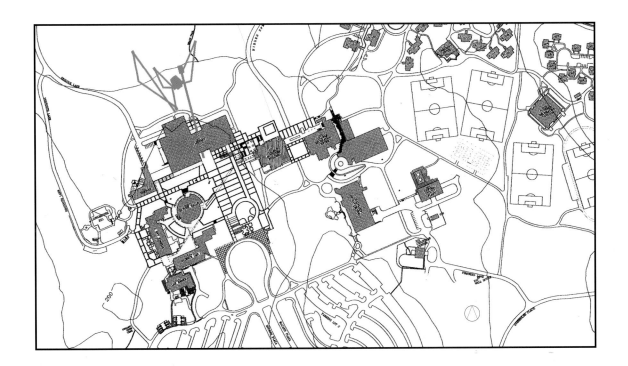

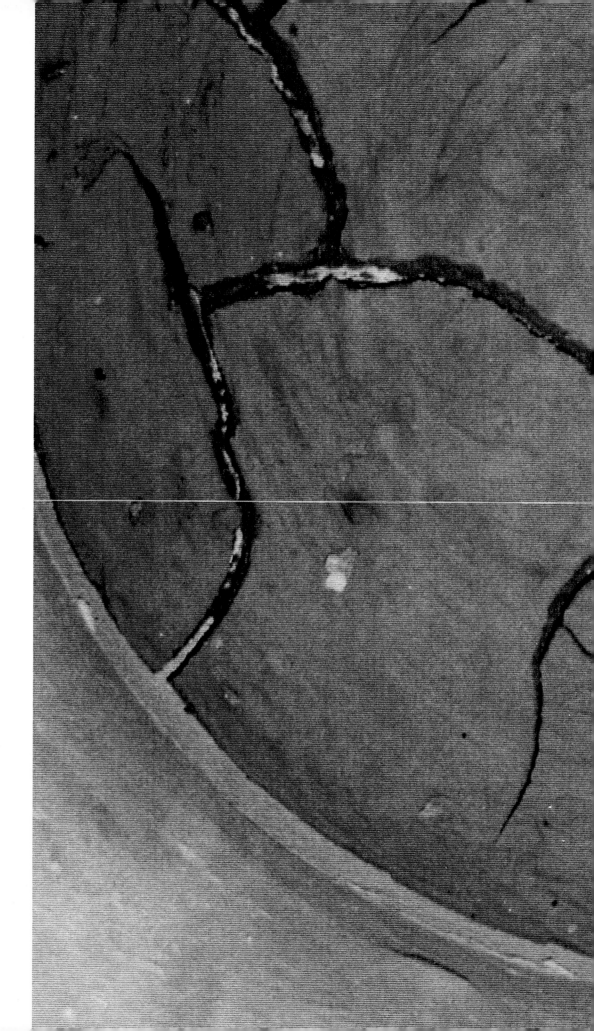

15400

PLUMBING

MudMap study testing soil conditions, moisture, and thermal cracking characteristics.

1 LIQUID SPACE

...ESSARY, DRAIN SYSTEM. UNFOLDING ALL OF THE WATER AND SPROUT. THIS ADDITIONAL SPOUT SHOULD BE PROPERLY DISPOSED OF BY ASSURING DOWN DRAIN WITH PLENTY OF WATER. IF COMPRESSED AIR CAN BE USED TO DRAIN THE SYSTEM, IT WOULD MAKE THE TAKE-DOWN OF THE BLADDERS EASIER. OTHERWISE IT CAN BE DRAINED USING GRAVITY. **EIGHT** DISCONNECT CIRCULATING WATER SUPPLY AT AIR RELEASE VALVE. UNBOLT TOP OF BLADDER, SAVE NUTS AND BOLTS IN A SEPARATE CONTAINER. **NINE** RELEASE AIR OUT OF THE INNER BAG THROUGH THE WATER HOSE VALVE. **TEN** CLOSE VALVE AFTER ALL AIR IS RELEASED. **ELEVEN** IF BLADDER IS SMALL ENOUGH AT THIS POINT, SLIP SUPPORT RING OVER THE TOP OF THE BLADDER AND CAREFULLY LAY THE BLADDER ON ITS SIDE. IF THE BLADDER IS STILL TOO LARGE, RELEASE AIR FROM SOME OF THE INNER BLADDER TUBES UNTIL THE RING CAN EASILY BE LIFTED OVER THE TOP. **TWELVE** THE COLD BLADDER HAS AIR ONLY IN THE LARGE CENTRAL BAG. THERE IS A LOT MORE WEIGHT—UNCONTROLLABLE WEIGHT—IN THE HOT BLADDER; CARE MUST BE TAKEN SO THAT IT DOES NOT TEAR ITSELF APART OR HURT SOMEONE OR DAMAGE THE GRID. AFTER EMPTYING THE AIR FROM ALL OF THE TUBES, THE CENTER BAG OF THE HOT BLADDER CAN BE DRAINED USING A SIPHON PUMP. (NOTE: A COPY WAS LEFT DESCRIBING AND PICTURING THE PUMP, AS WELL AS A SPECIAL HOSE FITTING FOR ATTACHING TO THE BAGS). **THIRTEEN** AFTER WATER HAS BEEN REMOVED, THE ENTIRE GIRDLE CORE CAN BE REMOVED (CLOTH JACKET AND ALL CONTENTS) FROM RUBBER BAG. **FOURTEEN** THE RUBBER BLADDER BAG WITH SIDES STILL BOLTED TOGETHER CAN BE FOLDED, WRAPPED CAREFULLY IN THE ORANGE AND YELLOW HEAVY VINYL CLOTH, AND PACKED IN BURLAP BAGS FOR SHIPPING. THERE ARE TWO BOXES FOR THE VINYL TUBING AND LARGE INNER BLADDERS. WRAP WITH PACKING MATERIAL TO KEEP INNER VINYL BLADDERS PROTECTED. **FIFTEEN** LARGE CENTER BAG SHOULD BE REMOVED, WELL DRAINED OF AIR AND WATER, AND FOLDED FOR SHIPPING. **SIXTEEN** CIRCULATING TUBING SHOULD THEN BE REMOVED FROM TIE DOWNS BY UNTYING OR CUTTING WHERE NECESSARY. **SEVENTEEN** TUBING TO BE RETURNED TO ALASKA RUBBER SUPPLY. FULL 200-FOOT LENGTHS SHOULD BE ROLLED ON SPOOL. OTHER TUBING SHOULD BE COILED AND BOXED FOR SHIPPING TO JET CONSTRUCTION. **EIGHTEEN** THE REMAINING GIRDLE CORE AND VINYL TUBES CAN BE FOLDED TOGETHER AND READIED FOR SHIPPING. (NOTE: IF THE TUBES IN THE JACKET ARE TOO DIFFICULT TO HANDLE, THEY CAN BE REMOVED AND SHIPPED SEPARATELY). ...

FACING PAGE: INFRA-RED VIDEO STILLS OF HUMAN INTERACTION WITH HOTPLATECOLDPLATE. THIS PAGE: HOTPLATECOLDPLATE VIEW TOWARD SNOWBLIND AND TUNGSTEN-ARC HORIZON.

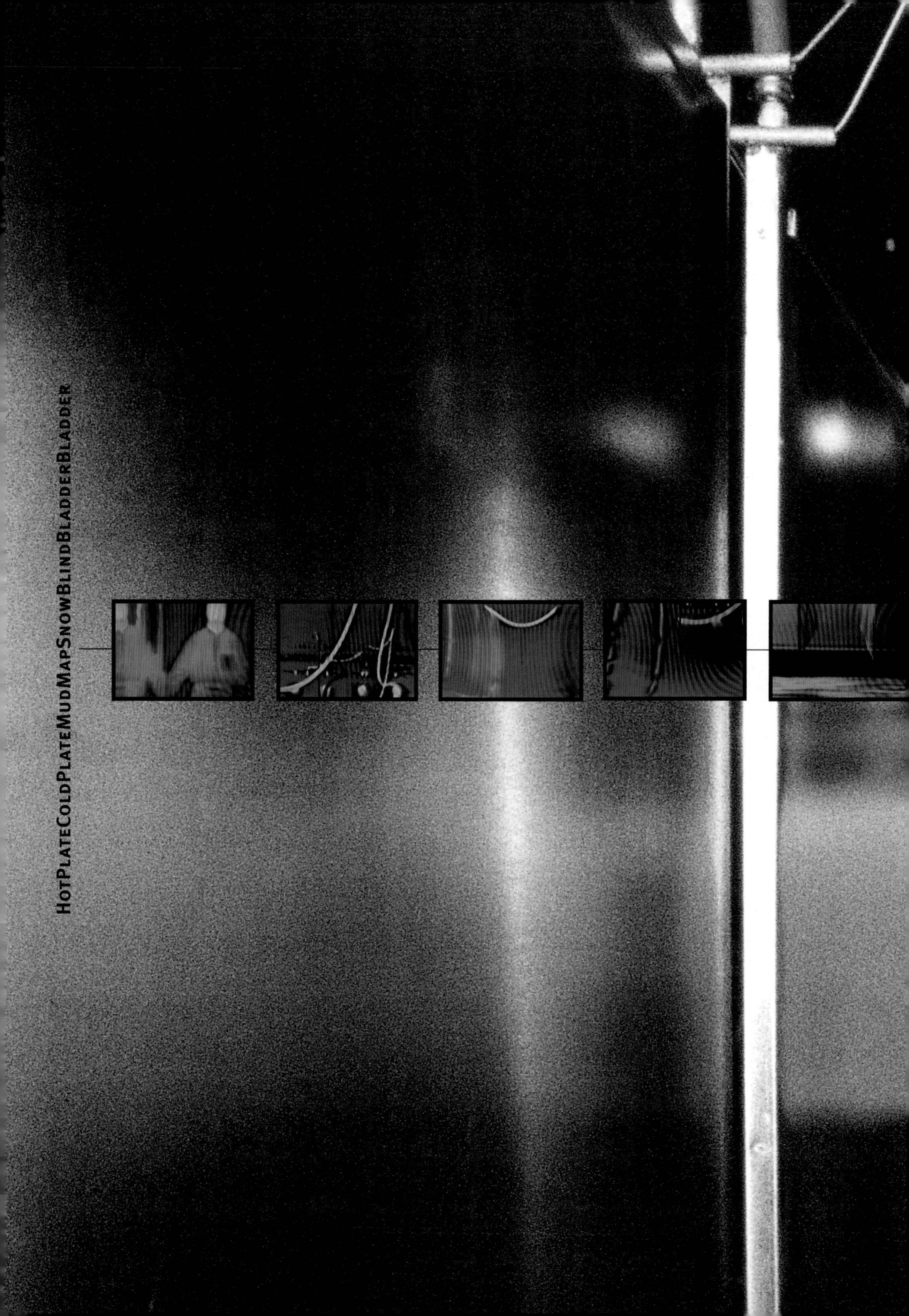
HotPlateColdPlateMudMapSnowBlindBladderBladder

The Alaska Design Forum invited us to Anchorage to create [00230] a project of imagination specific to this city. Fortunately, Anchorage is a distinct place, not in what is built there—which is generally as uninteresting and even destructive as just about every other recent American city—but in its blinding horizontal [13600] light; its encircling, smelly, salt water mud; its stinging cold and blazing artificial [15550] heat; and its many natural and manufactured envelopes of stored-away fat and gas and oil and steam and other elements essential to the preservation of life in this harsh landscape. We went there at both extremes of the seasons and imagined all sorts of possibilities for a new kind of urban design growing outward from the experience and responses of the human body interacting with this place. We didn't want to draw or diagram the essentially visceral approach that we imagined, so instead we built a kind of machine that we called HotplateColdplateMudmapSnowblindBladderBladder. We built this machine [15400] of stinky local mud and hoses and pumps and copper pipe and sheet metal radiator [05500] plates and chillers and boilers and two huge, pulsing, custom-fabricated rubber [06600] bladders, all set before a scrim of blinding whiteness slashed with a yet more intense halogen horizon, creating a light so bright that the machine and the mud and the world and the light itself became invisible, and only feeling was left. Then we filled this space of only-feeling with people milling about, intensely aware of the invisible light and mud and pulsing mechanical bodies, the swelling and sucking envelopes [15550] of heat, the gently drifting atmospheres, and pressures, and humidities.

Then we had this idea to use industrial infrared video to [11660] record this machine and the people milling around inside it. Looking through this big infrared camera, which is ordinarily used to find short circuits in power substations, we were amazed to see that in fact there was no space left in our machine for the people to walk around in. There was no emptiness left. We saw through the camera a space that was completely full, yet in continual flux, like a liquid. In this full, liquid space, the people were not discrete objects moving about among inert constructions. They were large envelopes of heat merging seamlessly with the heat of our machine, being [15550] sucked into its coldness and sucking its coldness back into their heat. Seen in this way, space had no emptiness; it was pure interactivity. Chemists and physicists already knew this. We began to think about the contrast with traditional and modern concepts of architectural space, which assume the placement of something (object) into nothingness (space) or else the carving out of space (nothingness) within something (inert solid). And we began to think about ways to carve and define a liquid space in [15400] which there can be no placement or displacement without simultaneous rippling consequence throughout a continuous material fullness.

DIAGRAMS

A FUNDAMENTAL WEAKNESS IN THE TYPICAL PROCESS OF DESIGNING CITIES IS THE OVEREMPHASIS ON VISUAL ISSUES OR ON ABSTRACTED ECONOMIC, POLITICAL, AND ENGINEERING DATA. A TYPICAL DESIGN PROCESS IS BASED ON DIAGRAMMING INFORMATION, MANIPULATING AND RECONFIGURING THESE DIAGRAMS, AND THEN ILLUSTRATING THE CONCEPTS WITH VIGNETTES. THE HUMAN EXPERIENCE OF A CITY IS OFTEN NOT PRIMARILY VISUAL AND CERTAINLY NOT DIAGRAMMATIC. IT WOULD BE WONDERFUL WHEN THINKING ABOUT CITIES AND DESIGNING CITIES TO UTILIZE THE NEW TECHNOLOGIES OF OUR TIME TO WORK WITH THE FULL RANGE OF HUMAN SENSUAL EXPERIENCE DIRECTLY, RATHER THAN WITH ITS ANALOG IN A REDUCED, DIAGRAMMATIC FORMAT.

ANCHORAGE, ALASKA 1995
WITH CAMERON SCHOEPP

FACING PAGE: HOT AND COLD PLUMBED BladderBladder ASSEMBLIES.
THIS PAGE: CROSSING HOT AND COLD MudMaps TOWARD SnowBlind.

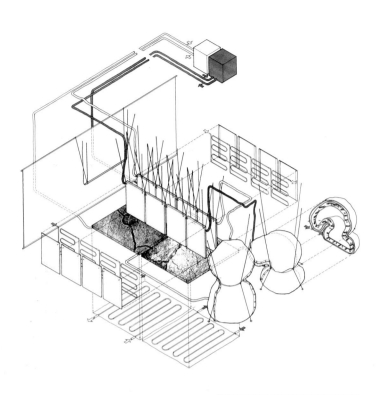

RIGHT: BLADDER RESTRAINT ASSEMBLY DETAIL.

JET CONSTRUCTION AND ANCHORAGE

HotPlateColdPlateMudMapSnowBlindBladderBladder EVOLVED FROM AN INTENSE PERIOD OF THINK-
ING ABOUT POSSIBILITIES FOR THE CONSTRUCTION OF ANCHORAGE. IT IS OFTEN A PROBLEM AMONG ARTISTS,
AND ARCHITECTS IN PARTICULAR, THAT A GLOSS OF SOPHISTICATION ADHERES TO ANY COMPLETED PROJECT,
SHROUDING THE CLUMSY FITS AND STARTS THAT REALLY ENERGIZE A PROJECT AND SERVE AS THE TRUE BUT
HIDDEN LINK BETWEEN THE EVOCATIVE FIRST SKETCH (CULLED FROM A HUNDRED FIRST SKETCHES) AND THE
IMMACULATE FINAL PRODUCT. WE HAVE A GREAT INTEREST IN THE PROCESS OF CONSTRUCTION: THE WORKERS,
THE TRUCKS, THE CRANES, AND THE HEAVY EQUIPMENT. WHILE IMPORTANT, THIS INTEREST MAY CONTRIBUTE
AS MUCH TO AN IMAGINED HEROIC IMAGE OF JUST-BUILDING-STUFF AS IT CONTRIBUTES TO AN UNDERSTAND-
ING OF THE REAL PROCESS OF FINDING IDEAS AND ATTEMPTING TO MAKE SOMETHING COHERENT FROM THEM.
IN BETWEEN IS THE NEED TO TAKE A STEP, TO BEGIN FROM NOTHING. IT SEEMS IMPORTANT TO REVEAL SOME-
THING OF OUR PROCESS OF IDEAS, BOTH PRACTICAL AND UNLIKELY. AS IN MOST PROJECTS, WE DREAMED UP A
BIG, COMPLICATED WORLD OF POSSIBILITIES BEFORE THE INSTALLATION EVENTUALLY SIMMERED DOWN TO
HotPlateColdPlateMudMapSnowBlindBladderBladder, LIKE A RICH SAUCE REDUCED FROM A LARGE
POT OF BONES AND IMPOSSIBLE ANIMAL PARTS.

WE STARTED WITH A FEW SIMPLE IDEAS ABOUT HOW WE MIGHT BUILD SOMETHING IN THE MIDDLE OF DOWN-
TOWN ANCHORAGE. THE CITY SEEMED VERY CUT OFF FROM ITS WATERFRONT. THE WATERFRONT IS MUD. MUD
CAN BE THOUGHT OF AS SOMETHING UGLY, TO TURN A CITY'S BACK TOWARD, OR MUD CAN BE THOUGHT OF AS
SOMETHING BEAUTIFUL AND SENSUAL AND FULL OF LIFE. WE SAW THROUGH MAPS AND AERIAL PHOTOGRAPHS
AND IN PERSON THAT THIS MUD WAS SOMETHING TO BE CELEBRATED. WE HAVE ALWAYS LOVED MUD. WE HAVE
PLAYED IN MUD AND WORKED IN MUD AND MADE THINGS OF MUD. ICE CRYSTALS IN MUD ARE SOME OF THE
MOST BEAUTIFUL THINGS YOU WILL EVER SEE. ICE PUDDLES IN MUD ARE THE MOST SATISFYING TO SMASH.

IN ALASKA THE GLACIERS ARE ICE IN MUD. WHEN YOU FLY OVER AND LOOK DOWN YOU SEE MUD, THEN ICE, THEN
DEEP, DEEP FISSURES, AND THEN A BLUE GLOW WAY DOWN IN THE EARTH. MUD CAN HOLD THESE MYSTERIES.
YOU CAN ALSO WALK IN MUD OR ROLL IN MUD AND FEEL IT OOZE AROUND YOUR BODY. IT SEEMS BETTER TO BE
BURIED IN MUD INSTEAD OF IN DRY DIRT. BEING BURIED IN ICE AND MUD BOTH WOULD BE THE BEST. THE WARM
AND SENSUAL GOOEYNESS OF MUD, THE COLD CLEAR PURITY OF ICE. MUD AND ICE ARE CENTRAL TO UNDER-
STANDING ALASKA: THEY ARE PERHAPS A LIFE FORCE AND A DEATH FORCE OVERLAPPING; LIGHTNESS AND
DARKNESS; MUD AND ICE. MUD IS THE EDGE BETWEEN ANCHORAGE AND THE WATER. THE AERIAL PHOTO-
GRAPHS REVEAL HOW IMPORTANT THIS MUD EDGE IS TO THE CITY. SOME MIGHT SAY THAT THE MUD SEPARATES
ANCHORAGE FROM ITS WATERFRONT. BUT THE MUD IS BEAUTIFUL AND MUST BE UNDERSTOOD AS ONE POSSI-
BLE CENTER TO THE SOUL OF ANCHORAGE.

AT THE TIME OF OUR VISIT TO ANCHORAGE, WE HEARD A GREAT DEAL ABOUT THE PROBLEM OF DISPOSING OF
PLOWED SNOW. THE SNOW PILES DEPOSITED ABOUT TOWN WERE TOO LARGE TO MELT DURING THE SUMMER
MONTHS; THEY LASTED FROM YEAR TO YEAR AS BIG ICY LUMPS OF BLACKISH, DIRTY SNOW. WE THOUGHT THAT
GIANT SNOW BURNERS MIGHT BE A GOOD SOLUTION. AROUND TOWN WE SAW SMALL SHEET-METAL CHIMNEYS
COMING OUT OF THE GROUND, AND, ALTHOUGH WE FORGOT TO ASK WHAT THESE WERE, WE ASSUMED THEY
WERE STEAM VENTS DESIGNED TO PROTRUDE UP THROUGH THE SNOW. WE THOUGHT ABOUT SYSTEMS OF
STEAM, AND UNDERGROUND HEAT AND PIPES, AND THE CIRCULATION OF GASES AND LIQUIDS IN THE EARTH,
AND BLANKETS OF SNOW ON HOT, WET MUD.

WE SAW THAT LONG, THIN DELANEY PARK, WHICH USED TO BE THE AIRPORT BEFORE IT WAS THE CENTER OF THE
CITY, WAS A VERY IMPORTANT SPACE. AN EDGE OF DOWNTOWN, AN EDGE OF THE ADJACENT RESIDENTIAL AREA,
IT WAS A BIG GREEN PLANE OR A BIG WHITE PLANE FILLED WITH PEOPLE RUNNING AND PLAYING OR SKIING ALL
YEAR ROUND. FROM THIS PARK WE COULD SEE THE MOUNTAINS VERY WELL, BUT NOT THE WATER, SO WE THOUGHT
THAT PERHAPS WE COULD DO SOME WORK HERE AND FIGURE OUT HOW TO CONNECT THIS PARK THROUGH THE
CITY TO THE WATERFRONT. THEN ANCHORAGE WOULD HAVE ACCESS TO SOME CONTINUOUS CORRIDORS OF SOME-
THING EXTRAORDINARY, WHICH WOULD CONNECT THE PARK TO THE CITY TO THE MUD TO THE WATER.

SINCE IT IS OFTEN COLD IN ANCHORAGE, WE THOUGHT IT WOULD BE GOOD TO DIFFERENTIATE THE ATMOSPHERE
OF THIS NEW PARK-TO-WATER SPACE FROM THE REST OF THE LOCAL WEATHER. WE IMAGINED USING THE
UNDERGROUND STEAM AND WATER PIPING, EXTENDING AND REINFORCING THIS SYSTEM TO CREATE TEMPER-
ATE MICROCLIMATES THROUGHOUT THE CITY. TO CREATE A FEASIBLE FINANCING SCHEME WE DECIDED THAT AN
IMMENSE SNOW-BURNING APPARATUS—LIKE A LUMBER MILL CHIP BURNER—COULD BE ERECTED TO VAPORIZE
HUGE PILES OF PLOWED SNOW. WE WOULD TAP INTO AN UNDERGROUND GAS PIPELINE AND CREATE A TOWER
OF FLAME. SNOW WOULD DROP THROUGH THIS FLAME TO PRODUCE STEAM AND CLEAN BOILING WATER. THE
WATER WOULD WRITHE THROUGH HOSES AND PIPES UNDER THE CITY, HEATING STRUCTURES AND WATER AND
MUD. THIS GIANT SNOW BURNER WOULD BECOME A FIERY SYMBOL OF THE CITY'S DEFIANCE OF NATURE.

DELANEY PARK WOULD BE RINGED BY A TRACK OF STEAM-HEATED SAWDUST FOR RUNNING AND WALKING IN A
WARM CLOUD OF MIST. TO THE INSIDE OF THIS TRACK WOULD BE A GLOWING BLUE ICE-SKATING TRACK, ILLU-
MINATED FROM BELOW, AND LASTING ALL SUMMER SO THAT ONE COULD SKATE AND SLIDE AND FEEL ICE UNDER
THE WARM JULY SUN. THE FLAT INFIELD WOULD BE COVERED IN GREEN GRASS IN SUMMER FOR BASEBALL AND
GAMES AND A PLANE OF WHITE IN THE WINTER FOR SNOW FORTS AND SKIING. IT WOULD NO LONGER BE ANNOY-
INGLY CUT ACROSS BY STREETS; TRAFFIC WOULD PASS UNDERNEATH BROAD, GENTLE ICE BRIDGES, DESCEND-
ING IN A SLOW ARC THROUGH A BRIGHT ICY GLOW TO EMERGE ON THE OTHER SIDE OF THE PARK. AT THE WEST
END A STEAMING MOUND OF FRAGRANT EARTH WOULD RISE UP TO PROVIDE VIEWS OF THE CITY AND MOUN-
TAINS AND WATER. AT THE EAST END OF THE PARK YOU COULD WALK BAREFOOT INTO A LUMINOUS ICEBERG
BEER GARDEN. SUNLIGHT WOULD GLOW EERIE AND BLUE THROUGH ICICLE STALACTITES AND YOU COULD FEEL
STEAMING HOT MUD OOZE UP BETWEEN YOUR TOES. AT THE INTERSECTION OF THE PARK WITH H STREET, A

ART AND THE CITY

IT IS NOT POSSIBLE TO JOURNEY INTO
ANCHORAGE WITHOUT UNDERSTANDING
THE GEOGRAPHIC AND PSYCHOLOGICAL
PLACE OF THIS CITY AS AN INSIGNIFICANT
SPECK OF HUMAN CONSTRUCTION WITHIN
THE VASTNESS OF NATURAL ALASKA.
BUILDING A SITE-SPECIFIC INSTALLATION
IN ANCHORAGE, TO BE ITSELF AN INSIGNIF-
ICANT SPECK OF CONSTRUCTION WITHIN
THIS CITY, STIMULATED A GREAT DEAL OF
THINKING ABOUT THE MEANING AND CON-
STRUCTION NOT ONLY OF THIS CITY BUT OF
CITIES IN GENERAL. ANCHORAGE OFFERS
NO REAL SENSE OF ITSELF AS A CITY
BEYOND ITS PRESENCE AS AN ACCRETION
OF NECESSITIES AND CONVENIENCES SERV-
ICING VARIOUS NOBLE AND IGNOBLE
EXPLOITATIONS OF THE ALASKAN WILDER-
NESS. THIS MUST BE TYPICAL OF MOST
FRONTIER CITIES, MOST AMERICAN CITIES.
BUT MOST AMERICAN CITIES THAT HAVE
GROWN WITHOUT A SPECIFIC CIVIC INTEN-
TION NO LONGER SIT SO SINGULARLY WITH-
IN A SOULFUL NATURAL LANDSCAPE.

THE CREATION OF CITIES IS AMONG THE
MOST IMPORTANT AND MOST FUNDAMEN-
TAL OF HUMAN ACTIVITIES, AND THE IDEA
OF A CITY DEFINES THE WILDERNESS
AROUND IT MORE THAN THE WILDERNESS
CAN DEFINE THE CITY IT SURROUNDS.
ANCHORAGE CANNOT REALLY BE A NEUTRAL
CONVENIENCE IN THE WILDERNESS AND
CANNOT COUNT ON A SOUL BORROWED
FROM ITS SURROUNDINGS FOREVER. A
CITY'S SOUL IS CONSTRUCTED FROM THE
INSIDE, SPECIFIC TO ITS PEOPLE, ITS
ACTIVITIES, AND ITS PLACE. OR PERHAPS
THE SOUL IS DISCOVERED RATHER THAN
CONSTRUCTED. OR IT IS BOTH. ITS DISCOV-
ERY AND CONSTRUCTION, HOWEVER, CAN-
NOT BE ACCIDENTAL AND CANNOT HAPPEN
WITHOUT THE HARD WORK AND THOUGHT
OF CITIZENS.

IT SEEMS LIKELY THAT CITY PLANNING
ALONE AS IT IS USUALLY CONCEIVED WILL
NOT PRODUCE A CITY WITH AN HONEST AND
ATTRACTIVE SOUL. A GOOD CITY IS USUALLY
REGARDED AS A GOOD CITY NOT BECAUSE
OF ITS PLANNING BUT BECAUSE OF ITS PEO-
PLE AND BAKERIES AND PARKS AND THE-
ATERS AND SCHOOLS AND HOUSES AND
BARS AND WORKSHOPS. IT ALSO SEEMS
LIKELY THAT A REALLY GOOD CITY CANNOT
BE BUILT IN LITTLE PIECES WITHOUT ITS CIT-
IZENS PARTICIPATING IN THE PHYSICAL AND
CULTURAL CONSTRUCTION OF A PARTICULAR
IDEA FOR THE CITY. THIS IS PROBABLY WHAT
IS CALLED CIVIC SPIRIT. BUT CIVIC SPIRIT
IS LIKE CITY PLANNING IN THAT IT SEEMS
SOMEHOW GRAND, ABSTRACT, AND
BLOODLESS, SOMETHING TO BE VAGUELY
"BACKED" BUT NOT LIVED WITHIN.

ART IN THE CITY IS OFTEN A CURIOUS
SIDESHOW ACTIVITY—AGAIN, TO BE
BACKED BY CIVIC-MINDED PEOPLE, BUT NOT
GENERALLY ASSUMED TO BE THE VERY
PROJECT OF THE CITY ITSELF. AS WE KNOW
FROM HISTORY AND RARE CURRENT EXAM-
PLES, CITIES THEMSELVES CAN BE GREAT

WORKS OF ART. YET EVERYONE NOW COM-
FORTABLY, OR SOMETIMES UNCOMFORT-
ABLY, REGARDS ART AS DISCRETE OBJECTS
MADE BY A FEW PEOPLE OR AS EVENTS
PLACED, AS OPPORTUNITY ALLOWS, HERE
AND THERE IN THE LARGE SPACE THAT IS
EVERYTHING OTHER THAN ART. THE MAK-
ING AND DEFINITION OF THE LARGE SPACE
THAT IS EVERYTHING-OTHER-THAN-ART IS
NOT REGARDED AS THE PROVINCE OF ART.
HISTORIANS MAY STUDY CITIES AS WORKS
OF ART, BUT THE BUILDING OF CITIES
TODAY IS ITSELF RARELY CONSIDERED AN
ART FORM. GREAT OLD CITIES ARE
THOUGHT TO HAVE BECOME ART BY VIRTUE
OF DESPOTISM, PRIMITIVE INTUITION, OR
RELIGIOUS EXCESS, BY THE ACCIDENT OF
LIMITED AND COHERENT MEANS, OR BY
THE ENLIGHTENED RULE OF GREAT MEN
WITH A DIVINE SENSE OF MATHEMATICAL
PROPORTION. SUCH CONDITIONS ARE
USUALLY NOT RELEVANT TO MODERN SOCI-
ETIES, MODERN ECONOMIES, OR MODERN
METHODS OF PRODUCTION, AND IT IS
ASSUMED THAT ART CAN BE ONLY ONE REL-
ATIVELY INSIGNIFICANT PART OF NEW
CITIES AND NOT IN ITSELF THE CREATOR OF
CITIES OR A CENTRAL PURPOSE OF CITIES.

THIS CONCEPTION OF CITIES OUTSIDE THE
REALM OF ART IS NOT VERY INTERESTING
WHEN IMAGINING THE POTENTIAL FOR ART
OR THE POTENTIAL FOR CITIES. IT IS LESS
INTERESTING TO THINK, "YES, ART DOES
CONTRIBUTE TO THE LIFE OF A CITY," THAN
TO THINK "YES, COMMERCE AND POLITICS
AND SCIENCE DO CONTRIBUTE TO THE LIFE
AND CREATION OF A WORK OF ART: THE
CONSTRUCTION OF A CITY AND ITS CUL-
TURE." IN THIS CONCEPTION OF THE CITY,
ART IS NOT JUST A SOMEWHAT GRANDER
OR MORE DAFT ACTIVITY AMONG THE MANY
DISCONNECTED ACTIVITIES THAT TAKE
PLACE IN THE CITY. ART OFFERS A CENTRAL
VISION, THE UNIFIED PURPOSE TOWARD
WHICH ALL ACTIVITIES CONTRIBUTE.

TALL ICICLE TOWER WOULD STAND AS A BEACON, HOLDING ALOFT THE ICE CUBE CLOCK. EACH HOUR THE MOUN-
TAIN OF ICE CUBES UNDERNEATH THE TOWER WOULD GROW AS A LICK OF FLAME RELEASED A CRASHING SHEET
OF ICE FROM ABOVE. THE ICE CUBE STACK WOULD BE SURROUNDED BY A MOAT OF MELTED ICE WATER TO KEEP
PEOPLE FROM WANDERING UNDER THE CLOCK AND GETTING CONKED ON THE HEAD.

WE DECIDED ON H STREET AS THE BEST CONNECTION FROM THE PARK THROUGH DOWNTOWN. A TANGLED TREL-
LIS WOULD LINE BOTH SIDES OF THE STREET AND HANG HALFWAY OVER THE STREET WITH LOOPS AND ARCHES
OF HOT WATER PIPE AND STEAM HOSES ENTWINED WITH BOUGAINVILLAEA AND OTHER EXOTIC FLOWER VINES
KEPT WARM THROUGH THE WINTER BY THE FLOW OF HOT WATER WITH HISSING CLOUDS OF STEAM AND
WATERED BY THE DRIP OF EVER-MELTING ICICLE LAMPS HANGING OVERHEAD. WITHIN THIS FRAGRANT CLOUD OF
HAZY HUMIDITY, SWARMS OF BUTTERFLIES WOULD FILL THE SPACE WITH GENTLE WAVES OF MOTION AND A RIOT
OF COLOR. CAPTIVES OF THIS WARM CLOUD, THE TROPICAL BUTTERFLIES WOULD REMAIN ALL YEAR TO REGISTER
THE MOVEMENT OF PEDESTRIANS AND TO STIR UP WAVES OF FLUTTERING DISTURBANCE THROUGH THE STEAM.

H STREET ENDS ABRUPTLY AT THE BLUFF WHERE THE EARTHQUAKE TOOK AWAY A BIG CHUNK OF THE CITY.
PEDESTRIANS COULD LOOK OUT AT THE VIEW TOWARDS THE WATER BEFORE DESCENDING ACROSS THIS
SLUMPED WASTELAND TO THE STREET BELOW. THEY COULD CHOOSE TO WALK DOWN THROUGH A MAZE OF
STEPS IN A TIMBER-SHORED ICE CAVE OR SLIDE DOWN THE HILL ON A SOFT RUBBER BAG FILLED WITH HOT
WATER. ON THE STREET BELOW, TRUCKS WOULD BE DUMPING PILES OF DIRTY SNOW ONTO AN IMMENSE, SLOW-
LY GRINDING AUGER SCREW BRIDGE CHURNING MOUNDS OF SNOW ACROSS THE TRAIN TRACKS AND WARE-
HOUSES TO THE INCINERATOR TOWER. ALONGSIDE, STEEL-PLATE PASSENGER PLATFORMS INTERLOCKING WITH
THE AUGER SCREW WOULD CLANK NOISILY TOWARD THE FLAMING, HISSING, STEAM-BELCHING TOWER, WHERE
THE SNOW WOULD DROP INTO THE FURNACE AND WHERE THE PASSENGERS WOULD STEP OFF. A GLASS-
ENCLOSED STAIR WOULD WIND AROUND THE INCINERATOR CORE. ONE STAIR WOULD LEAD UP FROM THE MUD
FLATS AND ONE STAIR DOWN FROM THE AUGER. IN WINTER YOU WOULD TREAD DOWN AROUND THE TOWER WITH
RED GLOWING STEEL PLATES AT YOUR RIGHT SHOULDER AND ICE COLD CONDENSATING GLASS AT YOUR LEFT
SHOULDER, CRACKING UP ALONG YOUR MIDDLE. YOU WOULD LISTEN TO THE DEATH THROES OF SNOWBALLS
RECYCLING INTO STEAM AND HOT WATER, SURGING BACK INTO THE LIQUID LIFE FLOW OF THE CITY, WHILE YOU
DESCEND ONTO THE CAUSEWAY, ACROSS THE MUD FLATS, AMIDST A TANGLE OF HOT RUBBER HOSES ROLLING
OUT TOWARD THE FISH PIER AND INTO THE WATER.

THE FISH PIER, A LONG, SKINNY, HALF-OPEN TUBE OF HINGED, OPERABLE GLASS PLATES SITTING ON THE MUD,
WOULD JUT OUTWARD OVER KNIK ARM. IT WOULD CULMINATE IN A GIANT SQUARE PLATE OF COLD GLASS AIMED
AT THE MOUNTAINS ACROSS THE WATER. RUNNING THE LENGTH OF THE PIER DIRECTLY THROUGH THE MIDDLE
WOULD BE A SPINE OF PERFORATED METAL GAS PIPE, LIT WITH A MILLION LITTLE LICKS OF FLAME LIKE A GAS
BARBECUE COIL. YOU COULD WARM YOUR HANDS OCCASIONALLY WHILE FISHING, OR TAKE OFF YOUR OVER-
STEAMED SHIRT TO DRY, OR SPEAR YOUR FRESHLY CAUGHT FISH ON A STICK AND GRILL IT TEN SECONDS OUT
OF THE WATER. UNDER THIS FLAMING GAS SPINE WOULD RUN A WATER SLUICEWAY FOR FISH GUT CLEANING.
OVERHEAD AND BELOW, STEAM JETS WOULD ENGULF THE ENTIRE PIER IN A CLOUD OF WARM STEAM FOR PLEAS-
ANT WINTER FISHING. LIT BY THE SPARKLING REFLECTION OF SUNLIGHT OFF THE GLASS AND WATER ON SUNNY
DAYS AND BY SODIUM VAPOR LIGHTS OF MYSTERIOUS ORIGIN ON DARK WINTER DAYS, THIS STEAM WOULD
APPEAR—VIEWED FROM THE BUILDINGS IN THE CITY—AS A TURBULENT AND LUMINESCENT CLOUD. JUTTING
OUT SIXTY FEET FROM THIS GLASS PIER WOULD BE THIN STEEL FISHING PLATFORMS HINGED AND COUNTER-
WEIGHTED SO THAT THEY WOULD DIP TOWARD THE WATER AS PEOPLE WALKED OUTWARD OR RISE INTO THE SKY
AS PEOPLE STEPPED BACK TOWARD THE PIER TUBE. SKILLFUL FISH HUNTERS WOULD CHOREOGRAPH THEIR
CASTING, MAKING SLOW, THRUSTING MOVEMENTS ALONG THE PLATFORMS. FROM OUTSIDE THE CLOUD TH
ARCHING, SILVER FLASHES OF THEIR CASTING LINES WOULD APPEAR AS A DANCE OF WHIRLING HIGHLIGHTS AND
SHADOWS IN THE STEAM.

FROM THE LANDING AT THE FOOT OF THIS GLASS PIER A FLOTILLA OF SQUARE CLUMSY BOATS WOULD FERRY
PASSENGERS TO THE HOT BLADDER ISLAND MOORED OFFSHORE. FROM THE BUILDINGS IN THE CITY ONE WOULD
LOOK OUT PAST THE FLAMING TOWER, ACROSS THE EVER-CHANGING MUD, PAST THE ROILING STEAM CLOUD OF
THE FISHING PIER, OVER THE CHOPPY COLD WATER TO A BLUBBERY, WHITE, IRIDESCENT, FLOATING RING
ENGULFED IN A HAZE OF RISING HOT AIR. LITTLE BLACK BOATS WOULD SWARM AROUND ITS BASE AND BOBBING
BLACK BLOBS OF JIGGLING, HAPPY PEOPLE FLOATING IN HUGELY INFLATED NEOPRENE JACKETS WOULD BE TETH-
ERED TO THE ISLAND WITH LONG RUBBER HOSES CIRCULATING HOT WATER.

THIS FLOATING BLADDER RING, FILLED WITH WARM AIR AND HOT WATER FROM THE SNOW MELTER, WOULD BE
THE FINAL OUTLET FOR THE HOT FRESH WATER CYCLING THROUGH THE CITY. IT WOULD EMPTY THROUGH A HUGE
RUBBER PIPE INTO THE CENTER OF THIS RING, WITH ITS CAPTIVE POCKET OF TROPICAL FISH. PEOPLE WOULD
ARRIVE ON COLD SUNNY DAYS, DROP OUT OF THEIR HEAVY WINTER SKINS, AND DIVE INTO THE WARM WATER
TO DART ABOUT EXPERIMENTING WITH THE INTERSECTION OF WARM FRESH WATER AND COLD SALT WATER.
SOME WOULD CLIMB INTO FAT RUBBER SURVIVAL SUITS AND BOB ABOUT OUTSIDE THE RING, BODY SURFING
THROUGH THE SWELL AS THE WARM WATER SURGED THROUGH THE HOSES CIRCLING THEIR BODIES, WHILE
OTHERS WOULD CLIMB OUT OF THE WATER TO BURY THEMSELVES NAKED IN THE WARM FOLDS OF THE GLOW-
ING BLADDER SKIN AND STARE INTO THE WEAK SUN AT THE HORIZON.

FIRST PUBLISHED IN SIMULTANEOUS LANDSCAPES: ALASKA JOURNAL OF DESIGN/CULTURE, NO. 8 (1996).
"HOTPLATECOLDPLATEMUDMAPSNOWBLINDBLADDERBLADDER AND THE CITY."

CLOUDS AND FULLNESS

2

ANDERSON ANDERSON

COMPETITION
MADRID, SPAIN 1995
WITH ANDREW ZAGO

PRADO MUSEUM EXPANSION

4-DIMENSIONAL PHYSICAL MODEL
OF PRADO SITE HISTORY.

11/25/95

Dear Andrew,

We need another level or another layer or time pulse of transformation beyond vegetable. Let's try the vegetable metaphor merged with the human body metaphor. We are not interested in the conventional metaphor of the human body as in Vesalius—the dead, external peering-in of humanist science. This needs to be a living biological metamorphosis into one symbiotic mindbody space—pure intellect merging seamlessly into physical sensuality. This is a completely fluid metaphor of the human body, beyond the conventional dialectic of mind and body, science and spirit, construction and nature, knowledge and feeling. We need to build one space of knowing: the mindbody.

The vegetable allows us to understand the space in which we are working, the pulpy medium into which we will construct the program of the museum. The membranous space of the vegetable is the dense, material presence of history, meaning, and spirituality: specifically Spanish culture.

The relationship of the museum to the city is analogous to the modern problem of the relationship of the mind to the body. The contemporary disconnect between mind and body or museum and city subverts the obvious logic of seamless interdependence and complementarity. The xeroxed section through the squash looks exactly like the map of Madrid. There is a clear reason for this. The seeds of the squash are the dense, transcendent centers of purpose within the large body of pulp. In the map of Madrid, churches, palace, and museums read as the dense seeds within the supportive pulp of the city fabric. If we zoomed in microscopically, we would find that both seed and pulp within the squash are linked through a living, writhing network of live, interdependent events. If we zoomed in on an aerial film of Madrid, we would see the Prado participating in a writhing network of live, interdependent events. This is not just a physical issue. In the case of Madrid, if not of the squash, the supportive pulp is not just material, it is also ideas, the palpable supportive tissue of culture itself. The problem with modern culture and modern life is the loss of our pulp. We cannot design the seeds, or live as a seed, unless we become reattached to some purposeful pulp. This is a spatial problem.

In most traditional cultures there is some external life-meaning beyond the individual person, event, or institution. This is clear in the map. The collective body exists to service the collective mind (culture), and individuals and the city fabric exist to service the collective cultural institutions: religion (cathedral), state (palace), art (museum), knowledge (university). Mundane life in the city fabric holds meaning in its service to culture. A traditional European city such as Madrid and a traditional museum such as the Prado have meaning in such a cultural conception. In a contemporary individualist culture Madrid and the Prado only have meaning as entertainment for individual visitors; the significance and meaning of the city and museum as organs of a living, progressive human culture is subverted. This is essentially a conservative critique of modern culture. There is a false conservative/populist dichotomy, however, and this illustrates the danger of exchanging simplistic politics for critical, specific thinking. Conservatism and popular entertainment centers both promote the death of living cultures rather than their preservation and continuing evolution.

The remaking of the Louvre is an example of transforming the museum into an entertainment center. This is not a populist act. It flattens and deadens and separates art from consequence and purpose. The question remains whether the Louvre, the Prado, or any museum as we know it actually performs its ideal cultural function as a living organ for the highest aspirations of the collective work of society. Does it ever become the physical evidence of the reason for a society's existence, provide the transcendent significance that gives meaning to living and working? Modern living and thinking and cities are complex and confusing. Current electronic transformations are giving renewed primacy to the mind over the physical realities of the body (although this new dominant mind space may be mindless in the sense of lacking internal critical structure). This reconfigured, supermodern mind/body dichotomy reinforces the disconnection. The mind we usually talk about is actually only one little piece of the

mind, the verbal intellect. In reality, the mind encompasses a much broader and richer and potentially revolutionary territory within human experience and creativity. This could be called the mindbody, which connects, stores, acquires, processes, criticizes, and creates a full spectrum of human experience—not all of which, not even a significant portion of which, can be assumed to be most usefully processed through verbal constructs.

The immediate point of this thought is to imagine the conceptual space for the Prado in relation to Spanish culture. The conceptual space that we imagine leads to a useful and perhaps easily developable physical metaphor in biology and the human body. This processing of our previous ideas through the layer of a specifically defined human body metaphor may result in the transformation we talked about on the phone yesterday. We can sidestep visions of the museum as either a center for popular entertainment or an elitist storehouse of socially detached, narrowly defined artifacts. The metaphor we have in mind is very simple. Maybe simplistic.

The site, literally and metaphorically, is the living, throbbing, membraneous pulp of the city. The site is the full, fluid, continuously interactive relationship of the existing museum buildings to their support and communications tissue, organs, and systems. The museum is the mind of the city, the memory center, and ordering structure for the city's creative enterprise. The body pulp of the city feeds the mind seed of the museum which carries the evolutionary DNA of the city's culture.

Ordinarily, a human body metaphor for the building emphasizes the mechanical service functions. This is of interest here as well. However, I think we should emphasize the mindbody conception in which knowledge, metaphor, idea, and creativity reside continuously throughout a physical, spiritual, intellectual, conscious and subconscious, natural and synthetic continuum. We're not just interested in the organs and arteries, we're interested in the subcutaneous pulp.
Mark

[THIS IS THE TRANSCRIPTION OF A SUBSEQUENT HAND-WRITTEN FAX FROM ANDREW WITH SKETCH DIAGRAMS.]

11/30/95

Mark and Peter,

What concerns me is that we don't have a radical medium. A section—as a design tool—preexists as a section regardless of what is designed with it. The same is true for a plan, a perspective, or a model. We need a medium whose relationship to plan or section is roughly analogous to the relationship of a movie to a perspective. Not only is a movie structurally different from a perspective, it also contains more stuff.

This does not invalidate the issues of liquidity and fullness. On the contrary, a radical medium is what prevents them from having any problem of being too literal. I also feel a medium development can be the most useful thing for us to work on at this moment. Otherwise, I keep thinking of buildings that look like fish or plants.

In a normative design process, the function is organized and then given a form that is more or less coherent, depending on one's talent and ideology. In a more progressive practice a form may be organized and a function made to adapt. I propose binary "form/function" units of design. Form/function units are not diagrams—especially the function part—but are visual things.

[DIAGRAM HERE OF ATM USE SHOWING DISTRIBUTION OF PEOPLE AT A SINGLE MOMENT OF TIME. THEN A 4-DIMENSIONAL MODEL SHOWING PATTERNS OF USE OVER A 24-HOUR TIME PERIOD.]

The pattern of people standing at an ATM machine is an example of an existing unit. The pattern changes depending on location, weather, popularity of the bank, and other factors. This reveals an uninteresting condition. If we turned around and designed that condition, based on, say, a pomegranate membrane/seed relation,

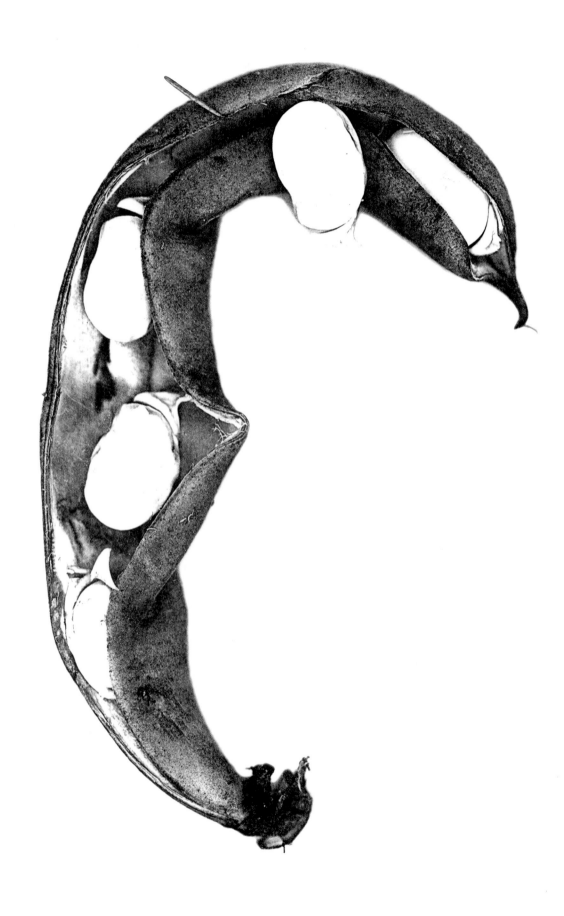

then we could have an interesting condition in which the pattern of use becomes the specifically designed space supporting the object of the ATM machine.

[DIAGRAM HERE OF POD-LIKE FORMS DISTRIBUTED ALONG THE 24-HOUR TIME CHART, WITH DISTRIBUTION OF PEOPLES/PULSES WOUND THROUGH IN THE SPACES DEFINED BY THE PODS.]

Combined with other form/function units overlapping in space, we could consciously design the membrane/seed relationship of the whole city.

Andrew

[FOLLOWING ARE EXCERPTS FROM MARK'S RESPONSE TO ANDREW. ORIGINAL IS HANDWRITTEN, 13 PAGES.]

11/30/95
Andrew,

Is the radical medium the design tool, the methodology? Or is the radical medium that you're thinking of a product, as in the medium of painting or a film? This is the peculiarity of architects, the confusion of method as medium (drawings, models, representation) and method toward medium (explorations by any available means towards another objective; the object medium toward which the method medium is directed). I'm not clear about the exactness of this distinction, only that the distinction is extremely important. It is not enough that our medium of exploration be made radical. To achieve a radical objective, a radical space, is a higher and more specifically directed goal than to achieve a radical methodology. A radical space could be explored and defined conventionally; a radical methodology might very well arrive at a conventional space. I've been trying to clarify this for myself lately after seeing a lecture by a vibrant, exciting, unconventional architect who produces disappointingly banal results. Such a waste of non-convention.

Anyway, I know what you mean. We also want to work in/on a radical medium and are most inclined to look for it via a radical methodology. I don't mean to belabor this, I just want to not lose one object for the other or allow the "space" of the computer, for example, as you were saying, to be confused with the architectural space that we may use the computer to look for. Would an ugly method possibly move us toward a worthy result? This is not unlikely. We have very little time for this project. Our immediate object is to produce a meaningful exploration. If we want to get anything done, we need to do this:

A. Invent/discover (not adapt) a radical methodology, a medium of exploration.
B. Focus this methodology on a specifically defined (even envisioned prior to exploration?) objective space. This is the scientific method: posit the theory, invent the construct to prove it. Radical objective.
C. (Re)present with (scientific?) clarity; Theory/Objective; Methodology; Representation. (The "artist's conception" is always distinguished from the "serious" work of the scientist/engineer).

Without having known where I was headed I have now written myself toward another of those crystal clear revelations that always hover a little way off in the fog, almost here, then, thankfully (if they are to remain hazy) disappearing so as not to torment further. What we need is a plan. A big radical idea with clarity and boldness. We can't stay forever in process.

I'm thinking of the people who decided to build the Golden Gate Bridge, the Hoover Dam. Modernism had certainty. We only have looking for something as our loftiest goal; not the construction of our vision, only the search for it. Do we want our work to be about looking? Or should we decide something and build it? Do we know something to decide, let alone enough about something to decide something correctly?

I'm running out of ink. I cannot think.

[CHANGES PENS FOR NEXT SECTION]

It is the unknown that is of interest here, and not the unknown that is the object of the search for knowing. This is the unknown that is accepted and celebrated as the unknown. We also don't have to be wallowing around looking for the big important thing to be discovered. We should sink comfortably (or maybe it is uncomfortably) into the certainty of not knowing and set aside the modern (Post-Renaissance) certainty of increasing knowing.

I think that El Greco painted this space or something like this space that we are no longer looking for but will simply sink into. In Renaissance Italy they painted knowing and in Renaissance Spain they painted the unknown. The Prado is not so Spanish. As a building and as a conventional museum, the Prado betrays the Spanish painters. It is too easy to say that this space is underground or that it is black. But certainly it is full. Full of the unseen. Modern people only know what is seen. This is very limited knowing. We should try to find an unseen architecture. Since we have eyes it will also be seen, but not only seen. We should concentrate for some time on what is not seen since we have several centuries of seeing to overcome.

Mark

[HANDWRITTEN FAX WITH SKETCHES]

12/9/95
Mark and Peter,

In developing the relation of fluid/site/fixed objects I thought it most interesting to think of the site/fluid collage as a snapshot of a dynamic system. To visualize it simply, I conceived of it as a diurnal wave beginning between the Ritz Hotel and the north entrance of the Prado, and ending near the Cason building and the Military Museum. As it moves it spreads and also bounces off some context, as shown in the diagrams. I am stymied as to how to introduce other elements. Every attempt à la fava bean/fluid collage is not nearly as successful. The results are surrealistic. You suggested an approach to it the other day (yesterday?). I would like to talk about that soon. Please let me know of the model, coordination is crucial.

With regard to the turbulence, I thought the main entrance could follow the trailing edge—i.e. there are a great many entrances to the new portions of the Prado, but when the turbulence overtakes certain ones, they become primary, while others close.

[DIAGRAM OF DIRECTION OF TURBULENCE AROUND MAIN PRADO BUILDING, INDICATING THE MANY ENTRANCES.]

In this way, the time turbulence and entrances follow the afternoon shadows. The last hours are by the Military Museum/Cason Plaza, which could house the assembly space and cafés and restaurants. In the morning it faces the bustling city, and that part is programmed accordingly.

The turbulence should be thought of in very broad terms. It can represent:

1) A moving (or pulsing!) built component
2) Movement of people
3) Daily variations in programming
4) Other temporary structures (shade tents in the afternoon).

Andrew

[SEVERAL SHEETS OF DIAGRAMS ARRIVE WITH ANDREW'S FAX, LABELED FRAME 1 THROUGH FRAME 8, SHOWING CHANGING CONDITIONS AT TWO-HOUR INTERVALS THROUGHOUT THE DAY.]

12/11/95
Andrew,

I know you think Peter and I have been thinking too much about objects instead of about space. I've been worrying about that a lot. It's not entirely true, but it's definitely a weak point. But anyway, here's another object approach. We couldn't help it. I think maybe we need to be abstract and spatial and also concrete all at the same time. We can use the object ideas that crop up as a way to figure out the space more purely once we step back from it. Otherwise, I think we'll get stuck. Anyway, here are some more object ideas.

We've been talking about the project in terms of time, and wave-like events washing across the site. Fava beans and pistons. How do we make the building physically react to the circumstances of time and event? Coral reefs are alive. Sea urchins excrete their architecture over time. They're a slug-like, pulsing membrane drooling out a beautiful inorganic architecture. We could build the air-interference membrane of the Prado esophageal infrastructure out of a material whose DNA has been synthesized from living organisms. This will produce a continually regenerative, variably permeable, living, breathing organ, excreting its own skin, and exhaling a healthy building atmosphere. It could be a photosynthetic material that transforms structurally, formally, and functionally during its daily life cycle. Here is a description of the construction elements sketched in the accompanying Prado at 2am drawing:

[NOTES BELOW REFER TO A LABELED SECTION DRAWING OF THE PROPOSED NEW BUILDING ELEMENTS CONNECTING TO THE EXISTING PRADO BUILDING.]

A. Breathing throat air distribution bladder.
B. Viscous horizontal walking membrane expands and contracts over time.
C. Hinged warped steel plate outer enclosure.
D. Extensible space containing bladder. Extends and retreats like a geoduck neck or scrotum. Diurnal time.
E. Thick, variable atmosphere mucus membrane.
F. Arterial-layered inner pulp—plumbing, power, communications.
G. Permeable, extensile penetration element. Historical time interface.
H. Geologic time earth interface lubricant.
I. Photosynthetic, regenerative earth atmosphere interface membrane. This building skin synthesized from living organisms.

Mark

12/13/95
Andrew,
Here are some additional thoughts on the ideas we discussed yesterday about building the organizing grid. Our sketches are overlays of the analytic drawings produced in Ann Arbor. I will describe the development of the sketch in relation to each of your drawings, referred to by color.

One: The specific point grid is developed from your one-way red line diagram. This point grid identifies nodes of specific activity within the streets and plaza. These nodes are diagonal with a specific magnitude of presence. A vector drawn through each node indicates the primary direction of the motion or line of influence generated by that node. The length of the vector indicates the assumed magnitude of influence generated by that node relative to the significance of all nodes in the field. The node grid is now no longer an abstract, unaffecting grid; it is instead a grid mapping of specific local spheres of influence seen as an interrelated field. The grid itself is activated. The grid and its geometry are not ideal and absolute. The grid is conditional and affected locally at the same time that it is comprehensive and universal.

Two: From the numbered plan showing the distributed building program, we have distended the program forms toward the activated local grid centers. The grid nodes are influencing the program forms with a specific magnitude and direction of force.

Three: Using the east-west grid developed in the blue line analytic drawing, additional points of intersection are plotted. These form a looser, incidental grid of point activities. This is the relationship we need to study most in developing the organizing grid for the project. The first field of nodes begins like a regular, abstract, imposed grid of classical, mathematical coordinates unaffected by the real world. That is how its points are initially placed. But once that grid is set into the specific spatial context of Madrid surrounding the Prado, that abstract grid becomes particular. It is the abstract modern/classi-

cal grid warped to a real context and then imbued by that context with specific attributes, forces, and relationships. But it is still a relatively ordered grid allowing itself to be read as such and creating a recognizable field. This new set of minor points is no longer recognizable as an ordered field of points. It is more like a cloud of varying density than a grid. These points are a mapping of specific events and incidents, displaced and understandable by circumstantial relationships internal to the context rather than by reference to an external ordering grid.

Four: The program forms are now warped and given a specific orientation and grain according to the specific attributes of the primary, living grid, and then they are locally warped by the circumstantial nodes floating through the site. Of course none of this stands still. The whole grid system and field of material and events is in continual flux.

Mark

12/15/95
Andrew,
Some of the juice from the geoduck and pumpkin sections leaked into our xerox machine. This project is starting to stink.

Mark

12/18/95
Andrew,
Here are the photographs of the physical model. We cut up all the sections. Toshi and Megumi spent all night weaving it. I started on it, but Peter and I are too clumsy and impatient. Just keeping track of all the spatial variables in the weaving was beyond my concentration. Too many telephones.

Watching them working, it was a beautiful process, so calm and patient and inevitable seeming. The model is pretty amazing. Of course by now it's pretty clear we're not going to have a building, right? But we have built the space of the project. In three dimensions. As a cloud of everything within the site or affecting the site. Physical matter and conceptual matter. The shards of history blown out transparently, all at once filling the site.

The grid is entirely evident, warped and woven into all the other facts and ideas of the city. It's like a frozen moment of deep, three-dimensional film, a really dense, roiling cloud of full space. If we can build this cloud as a model, can we build it as a building? I have no ideas yet about this. We have several more of these clouds underway now. The next ones are all text. They may be too abstract, although more honest and rigorous. Maybe a problem.

Mark

12/19/95
Andrew,
Here is the text for the final boards. Mark and I tried to boil down all of the ideas of the project into the allotted space. It's kind of dense, but I think it's all really important stuff getting at the heart of everything we've all been working on and trying to figure out. Is it clear enough?

Peter

12.21.95

[TEXT PRESENTED ON COMPETITION BOARDS]

The design objective for this project has been to invent a coherent space organizing the perception and construction of the current elements of the Prado National Museum in Spain with the elements of its extension and replanning. We envisioned the project as a continually developing event within the cultural life of Spain and the city of Madrid. In this context the Prado and its contents are viewed not as a collection of historical artifacts, but as an ever-transforming constellation of temporal events linked with material form and human experience, reflecting and generating Spanish culture.

The dominant Western conceptions of space position material objects and ideas within ordered matrices imposed on emptiness. A contrasting view, well represented in Spanish culture and in contemporary scientific thought, suggests a world of temporal flux within a space of roiling fullness. In the former model, the primary focus of thought is on the pure interaction of objects and ideas within an empty space of abstract, unaffecting coordinates. Within the latter model, space is conceived as fully material—interacting with the objects, events, and ideas operating within it. This is, for example, the full space evident in the paintings of El Greco, where subject and figuration share a physical equivalency with the material and cosmological space of the painting. There is no empty space in El Greco's paintings. Primary figures and events merge seamlessly into a continuum of interrelated supporting figures, events, and ideas. Everything pushes back and forth, spiraling and distending within a cloud of space and time that recognizes no boundary between physical substance and spiritual substance. This subjective, material space of El Greco's work stands in contrast to the constructed space and rational cosmology of his Renaissance contemporaries and to the dominant trajectory of Western thought. Our project for the Prado creates a full space, unifying the discrete buildings of the Prado not only materially as a physical practicality for the contemporary moment, but also as an architectural manifestation of a powerful insight in Spanish art.

To create a space of all fullness without intervening, mediating emptiness, we defined particular forms and events by reference to a subjective local context rather than to an abstract matrix or ideal. We constructed the space of the Prado as a local cloud configuration of material and conceptual fullness—the fullness of history and potentialities, people, material, and events. This cloud achieves its grain and direction through interaction with the site and its immediate urban context. The formal particularities of the cloud have been discovered/invented by tracing local turbulences and interactions within the cloud, producing particularities plotted over the course of time. The material form of the construction both facilitates and manifests continual flux of material, event, and human creativity in the city.

PREVIOUS PAGES: MODEL OF PRADO MUSEUM EXPANSION. THIS PAGE: DIAGRAM OF PHYSICAL INFLUENCES ON PRADO MUSEUM SITE.

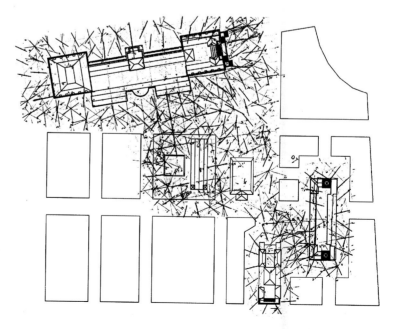

A BOMB IN THE SMELL PLAZA ACTIVATED
BY THE NOTE OF THE SHRILL HISSER AT
THE TOP OF AN EXCLAMATORY SURGE THROUGH
THE SWELL ENVELOPE SENDS BOTH
THE KING CLOUD AND THE PIGEON
CLOUD INTO WILD INTERACTION
AS A SWEET PUNGENT SMELL
CLOUD ACCELERATES OUTWARD
ACROSS MADRID AND NOSTRILS
FLARE IN FAR CORNERS OF THE
CITY IN RECOGNITION OF BIG EVENTS
AT THE PRADO.

SHRILL HISSER

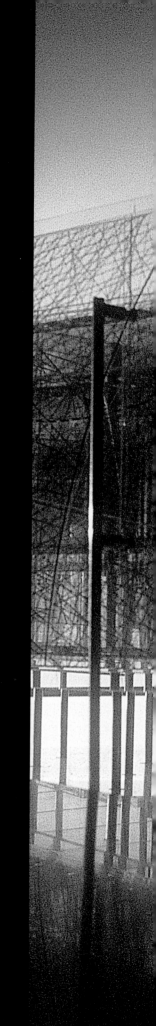

COMPETITION
KANSAI SCIENCE CITY,
JAPAN 1996

KANSAI-KAN NATIONAL SCIENCE LIBRARY

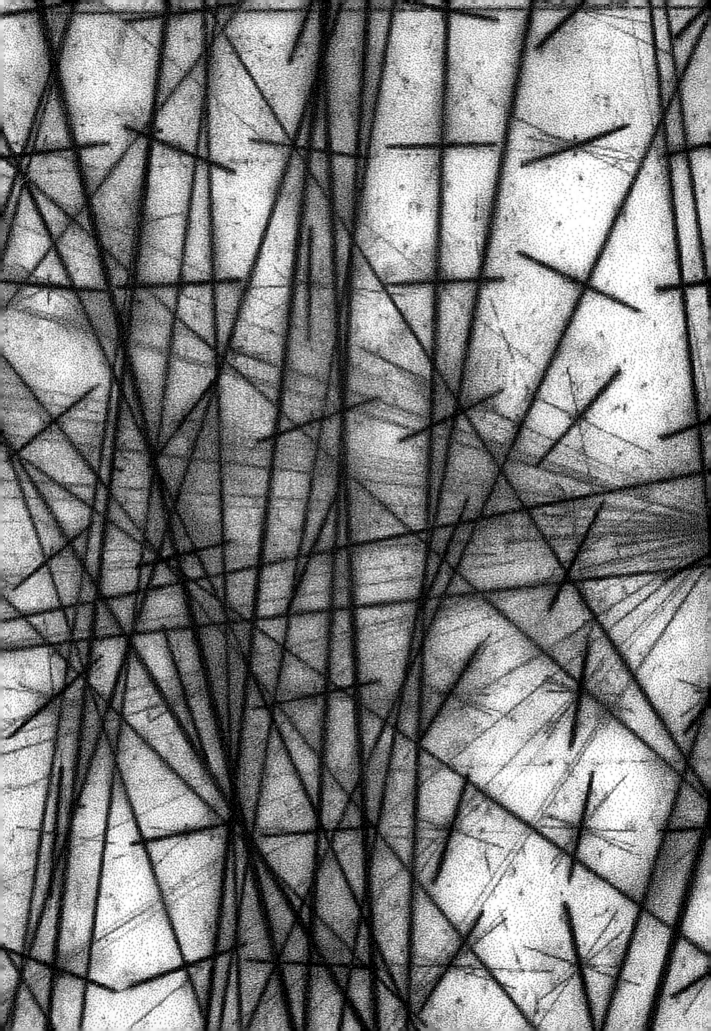

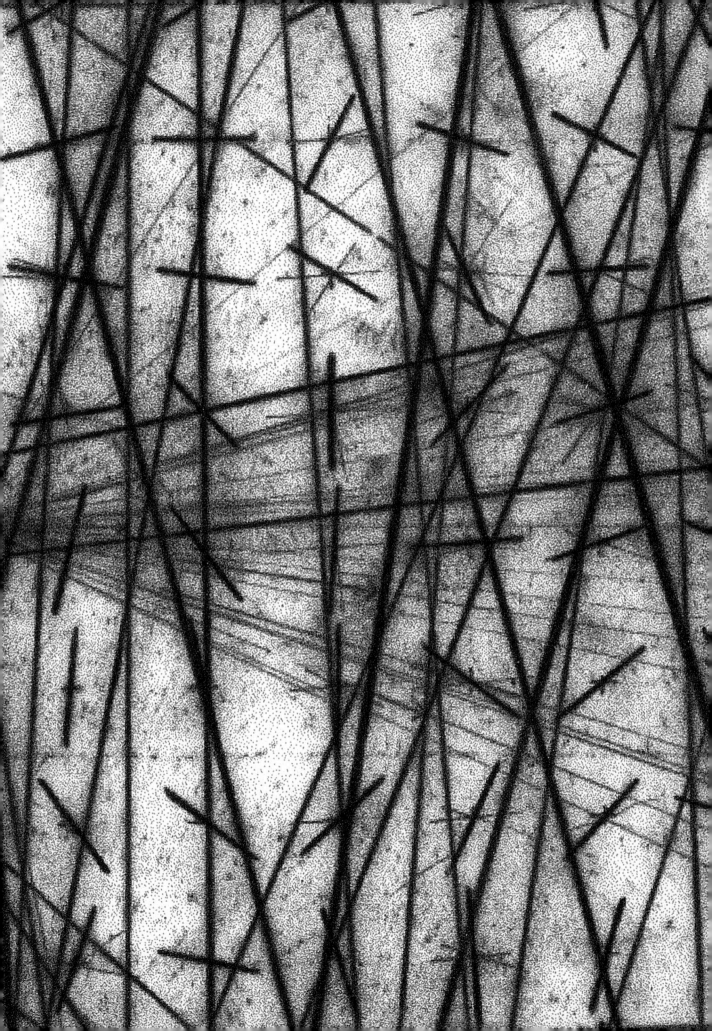

Libraries have always served an important symbolic function as centers of knowledge. Library buildings—typically solid, storehouse-like structures dressed as classical temples—have presented an image of safeguarding and enshrining the physical artifacts of knowledge. In the information age, knowledge can take many immaterial forms; the storage of unique physical artifacts such as books and maps is reduced in importance relative to the creation of access to new forms of non-physical information. The interface between user and knowledge comes not with access to the stacks full of books, but through a variety of tools that translate digital information into visible, audible, or otherwise apprehensible forms. Spurred by the rapidly changing needs of information preservation, storage, and dissemination in science fields, the Japanese government sponsored an international competition to solicit ideas for a new national science library. The site is a hillside in the newly created Kansai Science City, one of several "technopole" cities designated by the Japanese government to lead future developments in science and technology.

SHADOWS AND PROJECTION

ALONG THE SHORES OF PUGET SOUND, THE EARLY MORNING AND LATE AFTERNOON SUN SKIPS OFF THE WATER AND PENETRATES DEEP INTO BUILDINGS, PROJECTING SPARKLING ANIMATIONS ONTO WALLS AND CEILINGS. REFLECTED LIGHT HAS GROWN IN OUR CONSCIOUSNESS OVER TIME, PROGRESSING FROM A GENERAL APPRECIATION OF THE BEAUTY OF THIS PHENOMENON TO AN INCREASINGLY IMPORTANT DESIGN ISSUE. IN THE LOW LIGHT CONDITIONS OF THE NORTHWEST, WHERE CLOUDS IN THE MIDDLE PARTS OF THE DAY OFTEN OBSCURE THE SUN, HORIZONTAL LIGHT REFLECTED UPWARD FROM WATER OR WET PAVEMENT OFTEN BECOMES THE MOST AVAILABLE FORM OF NATURAL ILLUMINATION.

OUR SEATTLE OFFICE OCCUPIES A LONG SLIVER OF SPACE IN THE CENTER OF A LARGER BUILDING, WITH WINDOW ACCESS FROM A NARROW EXTERIOR WALL TO THE WEST. WE DIVIDED THE LONG SPACE INTO ZONES BY BUILDING TWO TRANSVERSE SERIES OF PIVOTING, STEEL-FRAMED GLASS DOORS. THESE SEPARATE THE WEST-END CONFERENCE ROOM FROM THE SHOP, AND THE SHOP FROM THE MAIN OFFICE AND DRAWING SPACE. A FREESTANDING GALVANIZED METAL BOX AT THE EAST END FORMS AN ENTRY AND RECEPTION AREA AND ENCLOSES A STORAGE ROOM AND STAIRS TO A MEZZANINE OFFICE LOFT. THE WINDOW OPENINGS AT THE WEST END OF THE LONG SPACE—WITH VIEWS OF PUGET SOUND, THE OLYMPIC MOUNTAINS, AND THE PORT OF SEATTLE—BRING LIGHT AND IMAGES DEEP INTO THE OFFICE. THE LIGHT PROJECTS ONTO AND THROUGH THE TWO GLASS WALLS AND REFLECTS BACK FROM THE SHINY METAL BOX AT THE OTHER END. DEPENDING ON THE TIME OF THE YEAR AND THE TIME OF THE DAY, THESE OBLIQUE PROJECTIONS CAN STRETCH ALONG THE ENTIRE LENGTH OF THE WHITE PAINTED NORTH AND SOUTH WALLS. FOR A FEW BRIEF MINUTES EACH AFTERNOON, THE SUN ALIGNS HORIZONTALLY WITH THE RAIN-SLICK UPPER LEVEL OF THE ALASKA WAY VIADUCT JUST OUTSIDE OUR WINDOWS. SHADOWS AND REFLECTIONS OF CARS, BUSES, TRUCKS, AND MOTORCYCLES ARE THROWN ONTO AND THROUGH THE GLASS SCREENS. AT THE END OF THE DAY, WE LIKE TO SIT WITH OUR BACKS TO THE WINDOWS, STARING INTO THE TRANSPARENT DEPTHS, AS SEATTLE'S TRAFFIC GRIDLOCK SLOWS THE VEHICULAR SHADOW BALLET TO A HYPNOTICALLY SURREAL CRAWL THROUGH OUR OFFICE.

We conceived of the building as a simple machine recording and condensing the ebb and flow of complex information washing across this site. An international center for the acquisition and ordering of humanity's knowledge of the natural universe, the library is constructed as a collector apparatus in the dense cloud of ambient knowledge and raw information that flows equally through the natural universe and the intellectual space of human culture.

The library is constructed of tubes within tubes of steel-framed electronically reactive glass walls, positioned between giant, electronically reactive glass partition screens. Activated by the pulse of passing communication signals, the building traces translucent electric shadows across the glass. These slowly rippling translucent waves become intermittent projection screens for randomly accessed data sets pulled from the library's active terminals. These pulsing electronic registrations and projections become intermixed and cross-shadowed with the natural projections of the sun and its rippling reflections off a shallow pool filling the ground plane beneath the elevated library tubes. Virtual information and natural phenomena become interwoven as a seamless physical event. Like the fuel cores in a nuclear reactor, compacted information massed as densely packed thunderclouds of published data hovers weightily within the transparent halls of the library. These heavy clouds of data breathe an absorbing condensation and explosive emission of critically assembled knowledge, scattering its projections and sunlit shadows like sticky pollen amongst the scientists and scholars, who swarm like a cloud of bees about their radiant, amorphous hive.

This space of flowing information becomes a wholly inhabitable material presence as physical and overwhelming as the now fading industrial space of smokestacks, furnaces, clamor, and sweat. One might stare down at this library from the surrounding hills with a perspective like that of a nineteenth-century farmer first glimpsing a fiery industrial town. The library is no longer a quiet storehouse of the past; it is an ambient turbine reeling in knowledge and spinning out the world's future.

PREVIOUS PAGES: STUDY DRAWING OF AMBIENT SITE INFLUENCES, KANSAI NATIONAL SCIENCE LIBRARY.

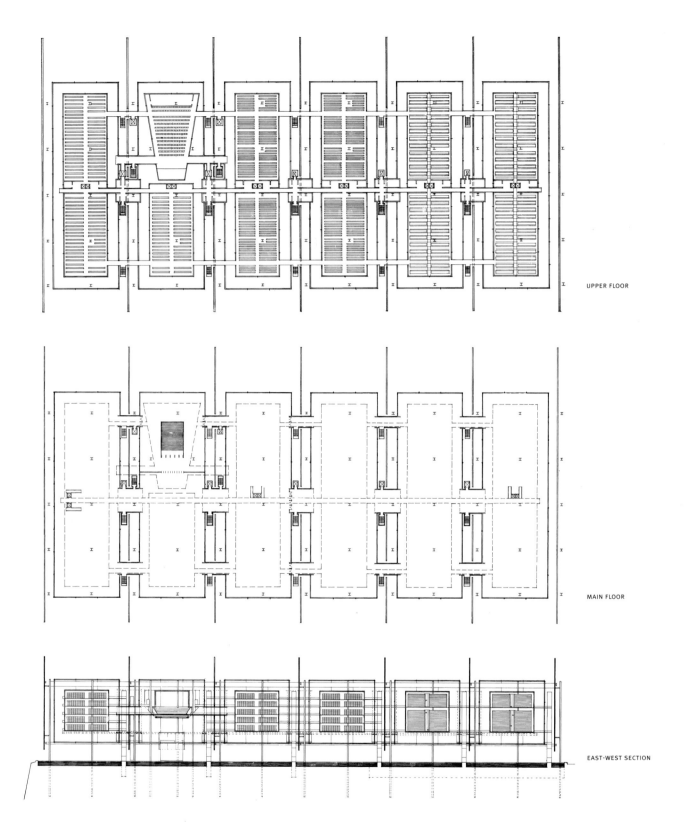

UPPER FLOOR

MAIN FLOOR

EAST-WEST SECTION

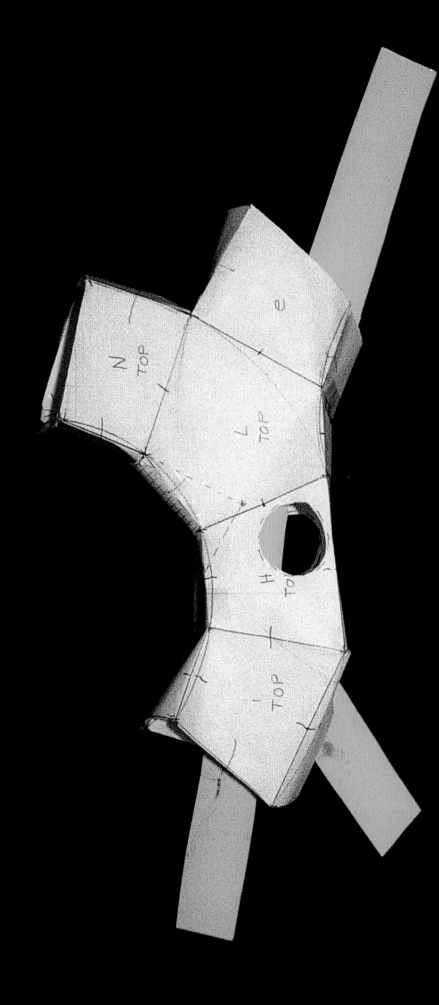

4 LIVE FILM

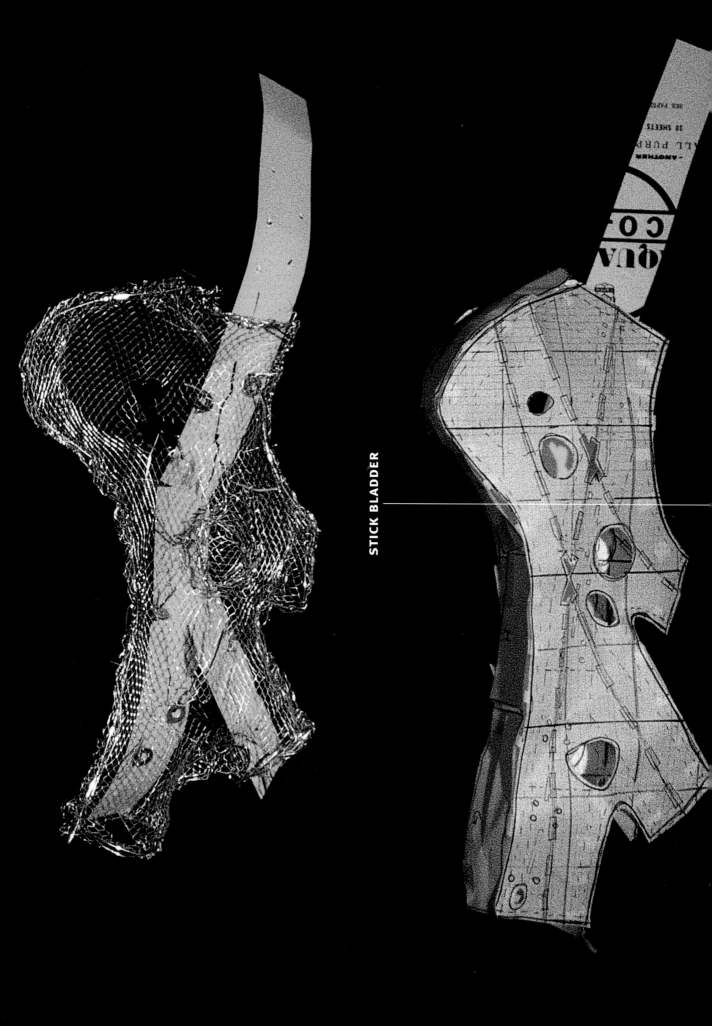

STICK BLADDER

Stick Bladder builds directly on the work of HotplateColdplateMudmapSnowblind-BladderBladder, and on the Prado and Kansai competition projects that followed it. We were interested in refining the thermal experience of BladderBladder and adding its element of infrared video documentation to this new work as a simultaneous experiential element in itself. We had been fascinated by the full, interactive space revealed in the earlier film, and we now imagined reaching into the video screen and drawing that liquid space out over our heads so as to become fully immersed in the space of the film. In many ways this was a muddier bladder project than the first.

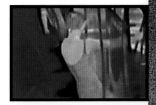

There are conceptual problems with mixing a simultaneous virtual representation of live experience with the physical event itself. Visual experience potentially overwhelms all other sensation. On the other hand, we are always looking into computer screens and imagining the possibility of walking into that space. How can we make that space physical? Pure virtual space has never really captured our imaginations in quite the same way. We are more interested in taking virtual phenomena into physical environments and seeing what happens when, for example, sunlit projections and shadows are mixed and cross-shadowed with artificially projected events, happening just beyond our usual visual wavelength. This was the main focus of our Kansai competition project.

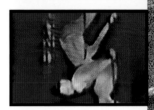

The construction was fairly simple, prefabricated at various places around the country and quickly erected in a tight schedule of 24-hour days between gallery shows. There was a welded steel, Y-shaped ramp holding damp slabs of mud heated with a network of copper manifolds and coiled radiator tubes. The ramp was supported on a forest of thin pipe columns rising from the floor, piercing through the mud and continuing up to support a soft, transparent, polyurethane cocoon enshrouding the ramp, a long string of sheet metal radiators, and an enormous internally plumbed black rubber bladder. On top of each stick of pipe an adjustable steel rod pierced the cocoon through a sheet metal washer welded to a structural mesh of steel cable cast into the polyurethane. To distribute the support over the skin—to avoid a rupture—each stick was capped with a fourteen-inch diameter red rubber washer, referred to as a measle.

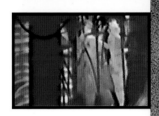

The skin was made in large, flat panels by laying out a grid of steel aircraft cable and welding it together with washers at the crossing points. A two-part urethane rubber was then poured along the grid of cables, allowing the fluid to flow outward, finding its own level—thickest along the cables, thinnest at the centers of space between the cables. This method created a varying depth and transparency of material, and left intriguingly shaped holes scattered across the panels. The varying transparency of the panels—ranging from opaque metal dots to empty holes—was essential to projecting multiple layers of live motion in the finished work. The sticky surface of the almost clear polyurethane was coated with industrial talc to create a powdered-smooth skin with a translucence suited for two-sided projection.

CENTER FOR CONTEMPORARY ART, SEATTLE, WASHINGTON 1998 WITH CAMERON SCHOEPP

The mud slabs were plumbed with a circuit of hot water hose, insulated below with a layer of sweet-smelling straw. The copper radiator cores were plumbed with cold water, so that moisture from the hot, damp mud would be sucked up and condensed on the cold sheet metal. The rubber bladder was constructed of many layers of material, hoses and sub-bladders of air and pulsing hot water to keep them supple, slumping, and attractive to the touch. People could move along the mud ramp, weaving among the steel sticks and radiators, bouncing against skin, measles, and bladder, inhaling strong organic smells and all the while dancing with their own infrared shadows.

Stick Bladder could be played with by individual visitors, but more carefully programmed performances were created by choreographer Crispin Spaeth and her company of dancers working with sound artist Suzie Kozawa, who played the materials and machinery and space of Stick Bladder as a musical instrument.

FOLLOWING PAGE: DETAIL OF CABLE-REINFORCED CAST POLYURETHANE BLADDER SKIN.

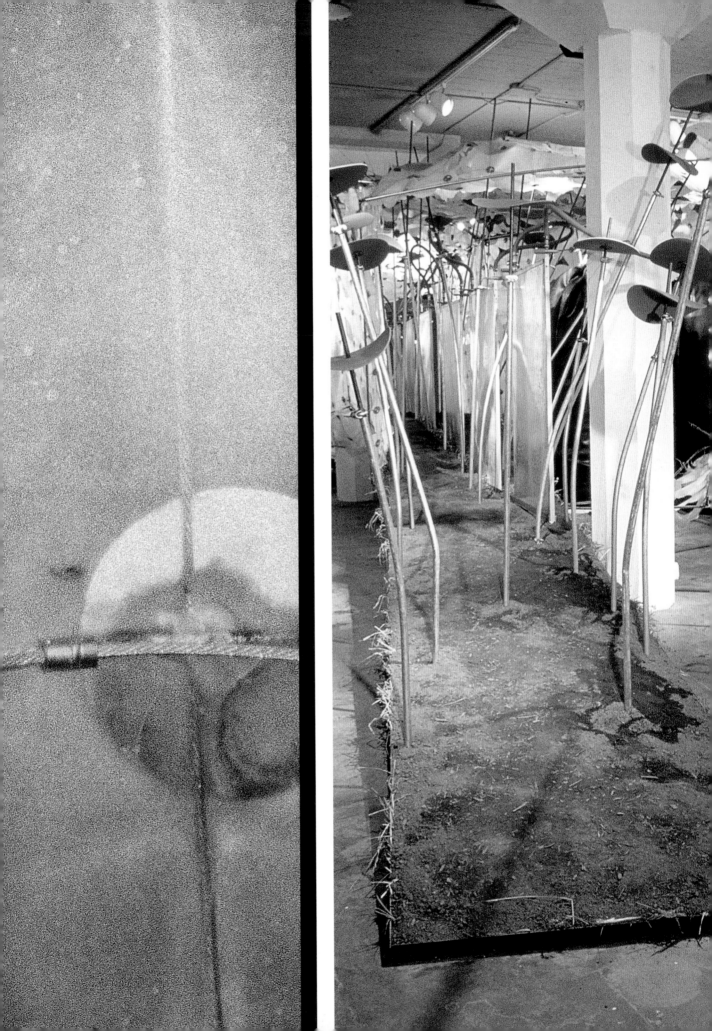

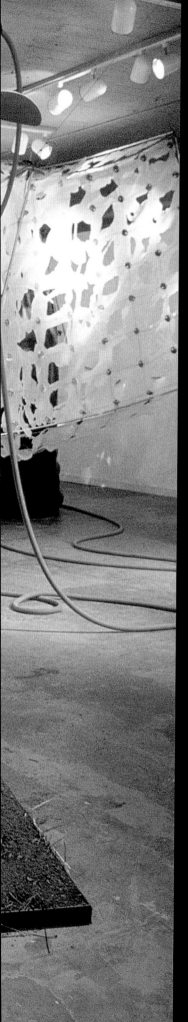

POLITICS, INFORMATION, CONSTRUCTION: A NEW FUTURE FOR THE HUMAN BODY

LECTURE PRESENTATION, SEATTLE 1996

The physical world is about to be sucked—brick, skin, and bone—into the cultural venturi roaring along behind the digital revolution. It is often suggested that rapidly advancing information technology and accompanying changes in public and private culture will lead inevitably to the marginalization of the human body's visceral experience of the material world. People welcome or lament this presumed demise of physical experience, but they rarely question whether it is a fundamental condition of the information age.

Politics, architecture, and the material economy share tangled roots in the natural and constructed constellations of matter, and relations between breathing, feeling human beings. The material foundations of all three structures—in all of their multiple and conflicting permutations, in their unique and in their interrelated forms and components—all face the common peril of substantive dissolution into the spiraling multiplication of unrooted, post-material shifts toward the primacy of virtual experience. The race is on for the economic commodification of all that is immaterial. With its infinite creative drive, business has long been evolving systems of economic valuation and transaction wholly independent of traditional concepts of capital. Capitalism will survive, and thrive, in a new economy set free of the limitations of finite material capital. Political discourse and political structures have dangerously disconnected surface information from material fact throughout history, but never with such alarming potential as in our current age of information.

Many architects studying the potential implications of the digital revolution foresee that cities will increasingly disperse, that human beings will have less frequent and less intense interaction, and that direct tactile experience of the physical world will be largely replaced or greatly modulated by virtual constructions created within information-processing systems. Yet at the same time, science and engineering have made use of computer technology to create entirely new understandings of the physical world and to invent powerful new means of exposing, displaying, and interacting with physical phenomena. Architects can use this new technology to build physical experience in radically intensified new forms, to construct a world in which the undervalued human body may create its own appropriate physical environment, just as the human mind is now racing ahead in creating radical new virtual environments. Cities may not disperse into increasing suburbanization, but will instead contract into rich condensations of architecturally orchestrated experience, simultaneously serving the visceral satisfaction of the body and the imaginative expansion of the mind.

Architecture cannot successfully stem the rising tide of apparent material irrelevance by standing fast in a traditional role. We must distance ourselves from a narrow conception of architecture as static structures defined primarily by reference to their surface context or historic lineage. Architecture has a broad, cross-disciplinary opportunity to merge into the flow of overwhelming future change, to revel in its liberties and new potential. It must not surrender to the virtual and conceptual at the expense of the material, but must serve as the committed bearer of materiality and physical experience through the transformations of a new age.

A REALLY COOL

ND ALSO HOT, GET-INSIDE-OF,

JIGGLY,

OOEY, MUDDY, RUBBERY, METALLIC,
ULSING, STEAMING, SLURPING,
SMELLY, LIQUIDY,
VIRTUAL/ANTI-VIRTUAL

SENSUALLY
NTERACTIVE
SPACE/OBJECT

5 AMBIENT INFRASTRUCTURE

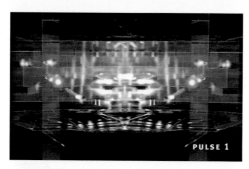

PULSE 1

PULSE 2

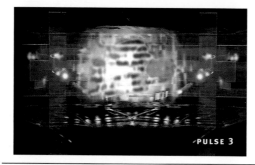

PULSE 3

SEATTLE, WASHINGTON 1997

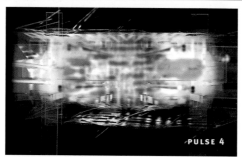

PULSE 4

PULSE 5

PULSE 6

TRAINS IN THE CITY

The San Francisco Museum of Modern Art commissioned a project from us, which was to be published in *Design Matters*. They didn't want an existing Anderson Anderson project, and for that matter, they weren't asking us to write any text. But Trains in the City is primarily a text project about viscerally experiencing the city. We produced many models, drawings, and photographs for the project, but the primary medium was an interactive construction specifications document.

The project we created had many simultaneous tracks, since we always tend to load onto any project everything we're thinking about and the kitchen sink as well. (You always need plumbing.) This project is an armature at every level, a minimal structure intended to be as invisible as possible, supporting a cloud of ideas and experiences. The project's conceptual armature has two primary tracks. One track involves the proposal of a series of train stations for the new light-rail transit system in Seattle. The other, and most important, track of the project concerns collaboration in the construction industry and the potential for creatively restructuring the construction documentation and communication process. The interdisciplinary nature of multi-media, four-dimensional, internet-based communication can breathe new life into construction documentation.

The current standards of architectural documentation impose a linear, fragmented, and often adversarial order onto the construction process. New information and communication technology, coupled with an imaginative reconsideration of the role of architecture in defining society's economic and cultural ambitions, can help us to recast the construction documentation's purpose and format. We need to harness the skills and creativity of all the people involved in the construction of a project. We need to regain a shared sense of purpose among the public, architects, and the construction industry.

These ideas parallel the administrative approach we have taken in affordable housing and prefabrication projects. As building contractors, we recognize that remarkable new materials and processes are less likely to have a major impact in the construction industry than minor physical changes affecting major administrative issues. Its for this reason that architects' fascination with elegant tectonics (a word we never use) frustrates us. We are as fascinated by materials, tools, techniques, and beautiful construction objects as anybody. It is wonderful that there is a renewed interest in the craft of building. At the same time, we recognize that the real frontier in our time is the potential to restructure and reorganize information and communication systems. What does this have to do with creativity in architecture and construction?

So far, there are two primary areas of digital focus in architecture. One area focuses on design and representation. This stuff is very sexy. We like it. The other area or track is intended to improve project management. There are all kinds of corporate architects flying around touting the amazing new era of streamlined, reorganized project management. They wear nice suits. They have ugly presentation slides. They talk about marketing strategies and big, bland, pretty architecture in Abu Dhabi and Seoul. But what if we got hold of that boring organizational software and used it creatively? We could blow the construction documents wide open. We could build a big, buzzing internet cloud of creative, interdisciplinary collaboration and still keep it all organized and more economically productive than ever. Couldn't we?

In the Trains in the City project, this second track focused on construction specification documents. Nobody thinks these things are remotely sexy. Contrary to logic, these documents are often the last thing created by the architect, a kind of mandatory afterthought often cobbled together by inexperienced interns who have no idea what they mean. They are the last thing read on the construction site, a document of last resort, primarily referred to when searching for arcane contradictions that may be used to obfuscate obvious errors: fearsome pages of dense, unintelligible text, layered in legal disclaimers, and treated by all sides like a stick of dynamite ready to blow financial ruin in all directions. Can such a document be reexamined creatively?

We envisaged the Trains in the City project as a sketch of an alternative way to work with specifications. To order construction information most rationally, we proposed using a system of hyperlinks within an electronic document, enabling easy cross-referencing across disciplines and systems. We have thought of this as a three-dimensional document that can be read in all directions. This structure places the primary emphasis on communicating the design intention rather than on specific information. Everyone on the job site needs to know the Big Idea. In that way everyone's knowledge and creativity can be harnessed to some objective greater than the successful completion of a small, circumscribed task. Everyone on a construction site is smart and has more knowledge of their immediate area of expertise than the architect. The architect needs to orchestrate all this knowledge and experience toward some larger purpose. It is crazy for the architect, or the salesperson who offers a pre-packaged specification, to write the arcana of a task without clearly relating it to the larger ambitions of the project.

In all of our project documents, we have been working toward systems that include the construction worker in our intentions. This is a simple matter of respect, but it is also one of enlightened self-interest. For example, take one simple and very common construction error resulting from a clerical transposition in a specification. Assume that a wall should be painted white. Many levels of decision remain to be made within the category of white paint. A diligent architect will research the sweeping complexity of issues related to white paint and then select Sherwin-Dutchboy 201XOP, instead of 211XSP or possibly POX112. Numbers may be transposed or incorrectly chosen at any point by the architect, the contractor, the supplier, or the painter. Without additional background, it is not unlikely that the painter will spray the walls with 211XOP. Perhaps it turns out to be lilac and someone notices the error right away, but more often it is the correct shade with the wrong sheen, or the wrong permeability rating, or has some incompatibility with the primer or substrate. The painter knows more about all of this than the architects, and may have been able to foresee the problem given qualitative information in addition to the model number.

We have learned all about paint the hard way. Our specifications now give the specific selection after first describing the context and the desired effect of this piece as related to the bigger picture. We usually request a sample and have a general statement welcoming alternative suggestions in relation to our stated intentions. This saves everybody time and money, avoids mistakes, and opens the process to a breadth and depth of information and experience well beyond the capacities of the design team alone. This is not a new concept. It is similar to the idea of a performance specification as opposed to a prescriptive specification. To take this to a deeper level, we would include facilitated access to information on other components affecting the element in question—all the parts of a construction system spiral outward in their effects upon one another. Most importantly, we want to figure out how to involve everybody in understanding the intent of the project—including the architects. If there is a blank on the specification sheet that asks what the Big Idea is, at least no one can escape the implication that there ought to be one.

Many buildings are only the sum of their parts. But architecture obviously seeks to transcend even the best relationships and functions of a building's parts. Oddly enough, there is no real place within any of the working tools of construction communication for explaining the high, transcendent purpose of the project. Nobody really knows what architects are thinking about, or how their work relates to the city, to history, to theories, ambitions, and big ideas. That's why architects only get paid for and sued for the little piece of their work that is reduced to a dry set of drawings and words with all of the big intentions washed out, set aside, even hidden. We hide our real work so well that many of the people in our own field work on only the parts of the building, and don't remember to actually work on the architecture.

Trains in the City works on one layer of the specifications problem. It is a sketch of the possibility that even the poetic intentions of a project might be embedded in the construction documents— hyperlinked with the nuts-and-bolts details, made available for the public and workers at all levels of the project to understand and contribute to the big idea.

SUMMARY OF WORK

GENERAL REQUIREMENTS: SUMMARY OF WORK 01010

SEATTLE WILL BUILD A NEW TRANSIT SYSTEM:
a 19th century passenger network tying together 19th century cities
and 20th century suburbs.
It will be built in the 21st century
when practical necessity no longer requires the movement of bodies,
since we can now sit at home, we are told, and bring the world to us electronically.

But we will still transport our bodies,
not of necessity,
instead for the pleasure of motion within the unfolding new world before us;
our bodies and our minds floating out sensually linked
within the new liquid space of a city experientially transformed.

The trains and stations and buildings and tracks
CONVEYING SYSTEMS: TRANSPORTATION SYSTEMS 14900
must accommodate the new role of the body 12100
as larger than before, a pulsing, transponding organism
floating out freely into the city,
merging with the space of its experience, merging with the space of its neighbors.

**THE NEW TRAIN AND ITS STATIONS AND RIDERS
WILL ABANDON THEIR 19TH CENTURY FORMS AND BECOME THE CLOUDS
OF A NEW EXPERIENCE IN THE SPACE OF SEATTLE.**

GENERAL REQUIREMENTS: REFERENCES 01090

The project is not simply to build train stations as we know them.
THE PROJECT IS TO BUILD SLOW PULSING CLOUDS OF HUMANITY IN MOTION.
The train stations are the enabling armature
for these constructed clouds of insistent human life
pulsing through the veins of the city and billowing forth
as large breaths of physical presence
pumped softly into the streets.

THIS DOCUMENT IS BEING CONSTRUCTED IN A PARTICULAR WAY.
WE ARE WRITING SPACE.

This new interactive and multi-channel construction document will merge
writing and thinking and reading
with the space of things and the space of experience.
We are inventing
a new way to write construction documents
and a new way to think
about building
so that we can read and write
floating in space,
travelling inward and outward
within the cloud of this page,
as we will float in the city,
forward and backward,
by this route and that route,
through the space of the idea,
outside of the line of a linear thought,
writing and reading and being and building:
afloat on the page, in the space of the project.
GENERAL REQUIREMENTS: MAINTENANCE 01800
WHO WOULD CLEAN ALL OF
THE GLASS AND EQUIPMENT OF
THESE STATIONS AND PUNCTUATE THE STATION CLOUDS
WITH LIFE AND DANCE
AND THE SAFETY OF NUMBERS?

There would be 3 shifts per day,
200 glass scrubbers per crew,
3 crews to each station.
EACH SCRUBBER WOULD BE CLAD IN SILVER AND MIRRORS
reflecting light
and scattering image;
scrambling rhythmically
across glass
on aluminum catwalks,

swinging in bungee-elastic harnesses,
scrubbing with hand, foot, head and butt;
with wildly tentacled pom pom sponges
of flashing silver and splashing suds.

**THIS MAINTAINANCE PROCEDURE WILL BE A CHOREOGRAPHED COMPONENT
OF THE ARCHITECTURE,**
integral with the space and merged with the weather;
a structural component of the experience of these breathing stations.
The project maintenance will provide neighborhood jobs that are fun
and that encourage a local pride and investment in each station.
The architecturally integral maintenance will keep the stations safe,
full of people, and full of the joy of motion and work and life.

13950 SPECIAL CONSTRUCTION: SPECIAL SECURITY CONSTRUCTION
There will be no ceramic tile salmon decorating dirty walls
14900 overwritten in Krylon
12100 FURNISHINGS: ARTWORK
"Return of the Undead Punks from Hell",
and smelling of urine
and nervous, last-century, frightened decay.

OUTLINE SPECIFICATION

14900 CONVEYING SYSTEMS: TRANSPORTATION SYSTEMS
ELECTRIC LIGHT RAIL TRAINS
01090 One system within an intercity, intermodal transit system.
02450 SITEWORK: RAILROAD WORK
Part way on the ground, part way underground.
Part way in the air
and finally on the ground again.
From the Northgate Mall to the University
through downtown Seattle
through Rainier Valley to the airport.
There will be stations on the ground,
and underground,
02300 SITEWORK: TUNNELING
IN TUNNELS AND IN THE SWELLING FOLDS OF PULSING BAROMETRIC BLADDERS
13010 SPECIAL CONSTRUCTION: AIR SUPPORTED STRUCTURES
buried in a gelatinous, elastic backfill.
02220 SITEWORK: EARTHWORK: EXCAVATING, BACKFILLING AND COMPACTING
AND BUILT ABOVE THE GROUND AS CLOUDS
05120 METALS: STRUCTURAL METAL FRAMING: STRUCTURAL STEEL
on thin steel columns
of variable dimension, composition, proportion and spacing,
01050 GENERAL REQUIREMENTS: FIELD ENGINEERING
calculated according to the microscale conditions of the site of each column,
02010 SITEWORK: SUBSURFACE INVESTIGATION
floating freely within the structural logic of site-specificity,
not marching, marching , marching dumbly
through the city to the numbing refrain of gross rationality.

AERIAL STATIONS

An outer tube of clear structural glass
08900 DOORS AND WINDOWS: GLAZED CURTAIN WALLS
woven together with an inner tube of translucent glass and structural steel
08800 DOORS AND WINDOWS: GLAZING
05100 METALS: STRUCTURAL AMD METAL FRAMING
with rectangular flaps cut from each tube, folded alternately in and out,
hinged and restrained
with motion damping springs.
13080 SPECIAL CONSTRUCTION: SOUND, VIBRATION, ANS SEISMIC CONTROL

**WHUMPING GLASS FLAPS RESPONDENT TO THE PULSING FLOW OF THE TRAINS,
SHOOTING INVISIBLE PRESSURES OF AIR.**

This station is not a miracle of modern engineering. It is mechanically clumsy.
An erection of structural and formal inconsequence,
this station serves only as an armature for the cloud of constructed experience
dissolving this quietly waving machine.

6 years before flying to the moon,
NASA astronauts explored the experience of weightlessness
by hanging from the ceiling with dozens of rubber bands attached to their limbs.

THE CONSTRUCTED CLOUD

SPECIAL CONSTRUCTION: BUILDING AUTOMATION SYSTEMS 13800
The cloud is constructed from the presence of people
recorded, digitized and reprojected as a sharp ambient mist:

SPECIAL CONSTRUCTION: RECORDING INSTRUMENTATION 13500
refracted, multiplied and intensified;
outsized and superextensile;
cast into the atmosphere (fog, rain or drizzle) through powerful lenses.

ELECTRICAL: LIGHTING 16500

THE CLOUD SWELLS AND SHRINKS AS A PULSE.

The clouds of sensed and projected human presence
collide gently skewed, conforming to still matter
and matter in motion,
wrapping fogs in the air, seeping through windows, disappearing as light.

An array of recording equipment. Broad spectrum sensors.

Rolling shoulders, swinging legs, a breath in the air.
Shivers of color rippling through space. Echoes in the atmosphere.

" I am laaaarge! ho ho ho."

I will leave on this train toward where I am
still laughing and rolling on the wall of this street.
"Mix with my memory, I'm swimming in yours."
Down the line in the future we have already met.

THE STATION CREW

These will be clean stations.
So that the continual wash of cleaning bodies sudsing the glass
will not register and broadcast,

GENERAL REQUIREMENTS: MAINTENANCE 01800
confusing the pulse of arrival and departure,

EQUIPMENT: MAINTENANCE EQUIPMENT: WINDOW WASHING SYSTEMS 11041
THE STATION CREW WILL BE CLAD IN METAL LYCRA
SUITS DENYING PROJECTED SENSATION,
except for a scattering polka dot static: hot tiny faces bobbing in space.
Silver sponges, hoses and soap splashing and wriggling across glass.
An army of sparkling ants swinging in harness, scampering weightless.
Many shadows through air, on aluminum catwalks lacing the glass.

EVENT

The train approaches.

A WALL OF PRESSURIZED AIR SURGES AHEAD ;
the building ripples, bristling.

The preceding ghost of the train runs through our hair;
a dry lick on the skin, the building swells,

WHOOSH!

The building breathes an inaudible roar in my ear.

An image bleeds forward ahead of the train:
a small stain of color, licking, absorbing, saturating.

FLASH!

ELECTRICAL: SERVICE AND DISTRIBUTION 16400
Sparking electric flame.
Rippling backwash pooling as pictures cast into space.
THE BUILDING BREATHES A RADIANT CLOUD.
Engulfed in the heat of exchanging bodies,

the cloud becomes a swarming hive.
Clean flashes of silver on hinged panes of glass.

13080 SPECIAL CONSTRUCTION: SOUND, VIBRATION, AND SEISMIC CONTROL
Structure dissolves in the images flowing:
inward, outward, multiplied, mixed and reflected.

13500 SPECIAL CONSTRUCTION: RECORDING INSTRUMENTATION

13800 **PULSE!** into the city.

Hot red humanity swimming in rivers of blue fluid air,
green in its backwaters, eddies and pools.

15880 MECHANICAL: AIR DISTRIBUTION

On the platform an orange is punctured.

I lift my arm, kiss blue, wisping, cold air with my lips:
clouds roll out swelling gently through glass.

A spray of orange liquid air.

PEOPLE, LARGER THAN THEMSELVES, BALLOONING,
merge as one great sea of color.
Bleeding with the chroma of life, rippling.

The smell remains. An invisible pungent cloud.

SPARK!

16400 ELECTRICAL: SERVICE AND DISTRIBUTION
The train pulls: slow building surge.
AIR SUCKING EYEBALLS. LUNGS ARE DRAINED.

The glass is clean.
Silver flashing pom poms. Rain. Dripping suds.
Dripping, dripping.
Sunlight, starlight, electrified mist.

Pooling image.
The station dissolves, surrounding us,
washing across the streets.
A TENTACULAR, OOZING PULSE:

01800 onto the walls and into the windows,

16700 ELECTRICAL: COMMUNICATIONS
reflecting in eyeglasses, windshields, wet shiny pavement.

The heat of humanity, liquid cloud of the train,
spilling calmly through the city.
Riders just left, riders remaining, riders arriving.
Enmeshed in the clouds of each other.

Fullness.
Emptiness.

Pulse.
PULSE, pulse.
A slow roiling cloud. Ebbing, flowing through the city.

PROJECT LIST

ENLOW 1998

ANDERSON ANDERSON SEATTLE OFFICE

1999

HART RESIDENCE	design; seattle, washington
OBATA 3 RESIDENCE	design; kosai, japan
HALL RESIDENCE	design; marrowstone island, washington
KUNIHIRO RESIDENCE	construction consulting; iki island, japan
NAGAO RESIDENCE	design; kosai, japan
ROE RAMSEY VACATION HOME	schematic design; hood canal, washington
TONN RESIDENCE	design; tacoma, washington
DETROIT DENSE SPACE	design; detroit, michigan
SCUMBAGDIRTCLODGASHUFFPHYTOCURTAIN	design and construction; tulane university, new orleans, louisiana

1998

ENLOW RESIDENCE	design; cle elum, washington
EVERGREEN FOREST CANOPY CENTER	design; olympia, washington
OBATA ZEBRA PROTOTYPE	design; washizu, japan
STICK BLADDER	design and construction; seattle, washington
COLBERT INFRARED SERVICES BUILDING	design; seattle, washington

1997

HOTA APARTMENT PROTOTYPE	design; chiba prefecture, japan
CHURCH'S ENGLISH SHOES STORE	design; seattle, washington
CLOUD ROOM (SITEWORKS OFFICE)	design; seattle, washington
OBATA SHOWROOM & OFFICE	design and prefabrication; washizu, japan
SCOFIELD MIXED-USE DEVELOPMENT	master planning; gig harbor, washington
TRAINS IN THE CITY	design; seattle, washington
WORLD HOUSE 2020 PROTOTYPES	design; japan

1996

HAMILTON LIBRARY REMODEL	design and construction; seattle, washington
IWAMA GUEST HOUSE	design; mount fuji, japan
KANSAI-KAN NATIONAL DIET LIBRARY	design competition; kyoto, japan
MORIMOTO RESIDENCE	design; tokyo, japan
NEDDERMAN WATERFRONT	design and construction; gig harbor, washington
OBATA OFFICE AND RESIDENCE	design; shizuoka, japan
PREFABRICATED APARTMENT	schematic design; nagoya, japan
SCOFIELD LEAVENWORTH RESORT	master planning; leavenworth, washington
SOPHIA HOMES ELDERLY HOUSING PROTOTYPES	prototype development; tokyo, japan
SCHOEPP/THORNTON RESIDENCE REMODEL	design; fort worth, texas
SUMITOMO/NICHI-HA TEST HOUSE	construction and consulting; bellevue, washington
TECHNOLOGY TRANSFER SEMINARS	development and presentation; kobe and tokyo, japan

1995

AMERIKAYA GARDEN VILLA HOUSES	design; tsuruga, japan
CECCANTI RESIDENCE	design and construction; tahuya, washington

HALL RESIDENCE, 1999

SMART TECHNOLOGY HOUSE, 1993

SMART TECHNOLOGY HOUSE, 1993

CHIYO NEW TOWN AFFORDABLE HOUSING — construction; kitakyushu, japan
COWBOY HOUSE PROTOTYPES 4-6 — design; montana
HO RESIDENCE REMODEL — design; gig harbor, washington
HOTPLATECOLDPLATEMUDMAPSNOWBLINDBLADDERBLADDER — design and construction; anchorage, alaska
INDUSTRIAL FURNITURE — design and fabrication; seattle, washington
OSAKA RESIDENCE FOR I.K. ESTEM — design; osaka, japan
ISHIDA FERRARI GALLERY AND RESIDENCE — design; odawara, japan
KLEIN RESIDENCE — design and construction; tahuya, washington
KOBE COMMUNITY CENTER — design; kobe, japan
LOEKEN RESIDENCE — design; raft island, washington
MARKEWITZ RESIDENCE REMODEL — design and construction; gig harbor, washington
MCCRACKEN RESIDENCE ADDITION — design; spanaway, washington
OBATA RESIDENCE 1 — design; kosai, shizuoka, japan
PRADO MUSEUM EXPANSION — design competition; madrid, spain
PRASTKA RESIDENCE — design; harstine island, washington
RUDIN RESIDENCE — design; port angeles, washington
RICHTER/WIENER RANCH — design; bend, oregon
WILLIAM & ZIMMER FACTORY/SHOWROOM — design; lihue, hawaii

1994

AMERIKAYA AFFORDABLE HOME DESIGN I — design; tsuruga, japan
BIG IVY AFFORDABLE HOME PROTOTYPES — design; sendai, japan
BLODGETT/GUILLEN RESIDENCE — design; gig harbor, washington
CARLBERG RESIDENCE — design; allyn, washington
COWBOY HOUSE PROTOTYPES 1-3 — design; montana
ELL RESIDENCE — design and construction; seattle, washington
ESS RESIDENCE — design and construction; wollochet bay, washington
GIG HARBOR OFFICE BUILDING REMODEL — design and construction; gig harbor, washington
HERRON APARTMENT COMMUNITY — design; nagoya, japan
LAKEBAY LUMBER RETAIL FACILITY — design; vaughn, washington
PALY RESIDENCE — design ; gig harbor, washington
PRAIRIE LADDER: EXHIBITION — design and construction; fort worth, texas
PIONEER SQUARE LOFT INTERIOR — design and construction; seattle, washington
RICHARDS RESIDENCE — design; gig harbor, washington
SHINOHARA RESIDENCE — design and construction management; tsuruga, japan
SEATTLE OFFICE INTERIOR — design and construction; seattle, washington
SOPHIA APARTMENT PROTOTYPE — schematic design; tokyo, japan

1993

ANDERSON RESIDENCE — design and construction; gig harbor, washington
BANKSON RESIDENCE — design and construction; wollochet bay, washington
FINLEY RESIDENCE — construction; gig harbor, washington
IVY COURT LOW COST HOUSING — construction consulting; sendai, japan
KENNEDY PROTOTYPE PANELIZED HOUSE — design and construction; gig harbor, washington
MARONTATE RESIDENCE — design and construction; gig harbor, washington
MULLIGAN RESIDENCE — design and construction; harstine island, washington
SMART TECHNOLOGY HOUSE — design and construction; gig harbor, washington

1992

DEVITA RESIDENCE — construction; gig harbor, washington
GIG HARBOR OFFICE REMODEL — design and construction; gig harbor, washington
HEILONGJIANG OFFICE TOWER DEVELOPMENT — joint venture proposal; shanghai, china
INTERNATIONAL INST. OF WOOD CONST. — construction consulting; tokyo, japan
KANAZAWA APARTMENT BUILDING — specification and shipping; kanazawa, japan

ESS RESIDENCE, 1994

ESS RESIDENCE, 1994

WeatherStation, 1992

Sullivan Residence, 1991

Nelson Residence, 1985

KOBE INTERHOME EXHIBITION — design and construction; kobe, japan
KLEIN RESIDENCE ADDITION — design and construction; gig harbor, washington
PRAIRIE LADDER: WEATHER STATION — design and construction; vaughn, washington
WOODFRAME LABORATORY — specifications consulting; tokyo, japan

1991
ANDERSON STUDIO AND WORKSHOP — design and construction; gig harbor, washington
BERTELSEN RESIDENCE ADDITION — design; tacoma, washington
BURLEY LAGOON PROPERTIES — site planning & development; burley, washington
CLOVER PARK CLINIC — design; tacoma, washington
DAVIE ART STUDIO — design and construction; vaughn, washington
MAYER/SCHEIDT RESIDENCE — design and construction; olympia, washington
MCCRACKEN RESIDENCE — design and construction; spanaway lake, washington
MAYER RESIDENCE ADDITION — design and construction; lakewood, washington
RUE RESIDENCE — design and construction; gig harbor, washington
CANTERWOOD SPECULATIVE HOUSE (2) — design; gig harbor, washington
STEILACOOM INN CONDOMINIUMS — schematic design; steilacoom, washington
STUEN GALLERY — design; pacific lutheran university, tacoma washington
SULLIVAN RESIDENCE — design and construction; gig harbor, washington

1990
AIKEN RESIDENCE — design and construction; gig harbor, washington
CAMP RESIDENCE — design and construction; gig harbor, washington
CHAKERIAN RESIDENCE — design and construction; gig harbor, washington
JOHNSON VACATION HOME — design and construction; harstine island, washington
KRAFT RESIDENCE — design; gig harbor, washington
MEYERS RESIDENCE — design and construction; port orchard, washington
RIPPERTON RESIDENCE — design; gig harbor, washington
SCHOEPP SCULPTURE STUDIO — design; fort worth, texas

1989
BUDER RESIDENCE — design and construction; gig harbor, washington
CHIAO RESIDENCE — design and construction; gig harbor, washington
YSIT DANCE THEATER SET — design and construction; university of washington, seattle, washington
FAIRBANKS SHADOW INSTALLATION — design; fairbanks, alaska
GIG HARBOR OFFICE RENOVATION — design and construction; gig harbor, washington
PRAIRIE LADDER: EARTHPLANE/SKYBARGE — design and construction; connemara conservancy, dallas, texas
THOMSON RESIDENCE — design and construction; gig harbor, washington

1988
ANDERSON DOCK & GREENHOUSE — design and construction; gig harbor, washington
HARSTINE SCULPTURE INSTALLATION — design and construction; harstine island, washington
HOLDEN RESIDENCE — design and construction; harstine island, washington
MARRONE/KRESGE RESIDENCE — design and construction; gig harbor, washington
SHADOWMAKER SCULPTURE INSTALLATION — design and construction; carpenter center for the arts, cambridge, maaaachusetts
TORSO PERFORMANCE/INSTALLATION — design and construction; radcliffe college, cambridge, massachusetts
WENTZEL RESIDENCE — design and construction; gig harbor, washington
FIELDING RESIDENCE ADDITION — design; wollochet bay, washington

1987
COWAN RESIDENCE — design and construction; gig harbor, washington
LEMKE RESIDENCE — design and construction; wauna, washington
METZDORF SPECULATIVE HOUSE — design; gig harbor, washington

Anderson Studio and Workshop, 1991

Marrone/Kresge Residence, 1988

SCREAMING BOX, 1985

TORRENS RESIDENCE, 1984

1986

FILMER RESIDENCE (SPEC HOUSE) — design and construction; gig harbor, washington
FRANGILO RESIDENCE (SPEC HOUSE) — design and construction; gig harbor, washington
FORT WORTH SCULPTURE INSTALLATION — design and construction; fort worth, texas
HOUSTON SCULPTURE INSTALLATION — design and construction; houston, texas
SPECULATIVE HOUSE — design; gig harbor, washington
TORRENS SMASH COLORS HOUSE — design; wauna, washington

1985

JERKE VACATION HOME — design; harstine island, washington
MARRONE RESIDENCE — design; gig harbor, washington
NELSON RESIDENCE ADDITION — design and construction; gig harbor, washington
SCREAMING BOX INSTALLATION — design and construction; harvard university, cambridge, massachusetts
WAUNA SPECULATIVE HOUSE — design; wauna, washington

1984

FOSTER RESIDENCE ADDITION — design; castagnetto carducci, italy
LEMARCHAND RESIDENCE ADDITION — design; vosves, france
MCMENAMIN RESIDENCE ADDITION — design and construction; wauna, washington
ROWLANDS RESIDENCE ADDITION — design; tacoma, washington
TORRENS WHITE FISH HOUSE — design and construction; wauna, washington
WILLIAMS RESIDENCE ADDITION — design; wauna, washington

design; tacoma, washington

1983

NORDBY RESIDENCE ADDITION — design and construction; tacoma, washington
SAM AND ALICE SCULPTURE INSTALLATION — design and construction; tacoma, washington
TORRENS SCULPTURE STUDIO — design; wauna, washington

1982

EYLER RESIDENCE REMODEL — design and construction; gig harbor, washington
RASMUSSEN RESIDENCE ADDITION — design and construction; tacoma, washington
TONN RESIDENCE GARAGE ADDITION — design and construction; tacoma, washington

1981

ANDERSON RESIDENCE ADDITION — design and construction; tacoma, washington
COMMERCIAL FIRE HYDRANT SYSTEM — construction; gig harbor, washington
FONTE FERRATA FARM PROJECTS — design and construction; castagnetto carducci, italy

1980

LITZENBERGER RESIDENCE ADDITION — construction; gig harbor, washington

1979

OTTO JAHN WATER SYSTEM — construction; gig harbor, washington

1978

LITZENBERGER VACATION HOME — construction; harstine island, washington

1977

ANDERSON VACATION HOME — construction; harstine island, washington
REIGSTAD ADDITION — construction; puyallup, washington

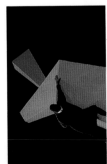

YSIT DANCE THEATER SET, 1989

AIKEN RESIDENCE, 1990

ACKNOWLEDGMENTS

Many people have contributed to producing this work and this book. We would like especially to thank the many employees, consultants, subcontractors, and creative collaborators who have been central to the production and enjoyment of the work we have done together. Martin MacDonald, Suzanne Knapp, and Titian Niosi were the core of our team during many important years building our construction company. Many consultants and subcontractors have been critical to our continuing education and to the development of our work. Among them Terry Nettles, structural engineer; Tom Edwards, lumber supplier; Mike Six, plumber; Mac Fields, excavator; Murdock Martensen, cabinetmaker; and Jean Jonas, accountant, have all been invaluable colleagues. Megumi Tamanaha and Masatoshi Kasai have contributed invaluable enthusiasm and talent during some of our most enjoyable and stimulating recent design projects.

Cameron Schoepp, sculptor, has been a creative collaborator on several of the projects included in this book. Frequently working with us under the group name Jet Construction, Cameron has been a friend and colleague on many important projects that we have undertaken since studying art together in college. We have worked together with architect Andrew Zago on numerous creative projects as well. Most importantly, our continual long-distance dialogue with Andrew on contemporary issues in architecture, culture, and our respective projects has been very important in helping to keep our thoughts focused and striving towards deeper ambitions.

Many teachers have contributed significantly to our work, as have, more recently, many students and teaching colleagues. We would like especially to thank Mordechai Rozanski, Christopher Browning, Paul Webster, Roberta Brown, Dave Suderman, Paul Reigstad, Tom Torrens, and Dave Keyes who taught us at Pacific Lutheran University; Marc Angélil, Frank Gehry, Paul Lubowicki, Coosje Van Bruggen, and Antoine Predock at Harvard; and Otto Piene at MIT. Recent colleagues Samia Rab, Pu Miao, Victor Olgyay, Bruce Etherington, Chang Qing, Jin Ho Park, and Stephen Meder have been appreciated friends as we have begun to learn to be teachers ourselves.

In connection with our projects in Japan we have greatly enjoyed working, teaching, and traveling with Roger Williams, Tom Ossinger, Izumi Kuroiwa, Ted Tanase, Mark Calhoon, Paul Boardman, Scot Simpson, and Ivan Eastin. Our work in Japan has been enriched and made enjoyable by long-term business collaborators, clients, and friends Mike Obata and Robert Yamazaki. In the project of starting the Space.City Art and Architecture forum in Seattle, we have had the chance to become friends and collaborators with Mark Johnson, Grant Gustafson, Amy Lelyveld, Laurel Wilson, Susan Jones, Anthony Pellecchia, and Kathy Wesselman.

Our installation and exhibition projects, including the work with Jet Construction, have received the support of many patrons, contributors, collaborators, and volunteers. We would like to especially thank Amy Monier of the Connemara Conservancy; Peter Lipson, Sar Schnucker, Margaret Donatello, Harold Wallin and the Alaska Design Forum; the Center on Contemporary Art in Seattle, along with collaborators Crispin Spaeth and Susie Kozawa, and the technical support of Fred Colbert, Microsoft, Boeing, and the Henry Art Museum; Aaron Betsky and the San Francisco Museum of Modern Art; Greg Tsark, Felipe Correa, Kala Yasuda, Sugar Goatee (the band), and the architecture students of Tulane University and the University of Hawaii.

We could have done very little work at all without the confidence and support of our many clients. We must thank most of them as a group, but would like especially to mention Suzanne and Peter Sullivan, and George and Edie Rue, who have been continuous supporters of our work and gracious hosts to visitors. Mike Marrone and Kathy Kresge, Rick and Peggy Johnson, Joanne and Richard Klein, Sheri and Jeff Tonn, Itaru and Miho Ishida, and Clair Enlow have worked with us through projects that opened new directions at critical times in our work. Architect Ted Litzenberger was our first construction client and taught us by example many lessons about the entrepreneurial role of making things in the creative practice of architecture. Our time spent with Edie Foster on her farm in Italy has provided a lasting influence on us and our work. Nalini Nadkarni has become our fellow traveler in new and unfinished adventures exploring relationships between architecture, science, and nature, opening our eyes to ideas and spaces we never knew existed.

This book has come to be produced only through the talent, hard work, and patience of its editor, Jan Cigliano, and her colleagues at Princeton Architectural Press. We especially appreciate the initiation of the project through the recommendations and encouragement of Beth Dunlop and Sheri Olson. Anne Bush has been not only the book designer, but also a friend, critic, and collaborator through all phases of this project. Additional contributors include Michael Scarbrough, for his valued photography, and Marilyn Davie and John Zuern, for their readings and criticism of our writing.

Above all, we would like to thank our parents, Charles and Margaret Anderson, who have generously filled at one time or another every role of collaborator, teacher, mentor, colleague, assistant, editor, client, and friend listed above. This book is dedicated to our parents, and to Kristi.

DESIGN AND CONSTRUCTION TEAM 1984-2000

Mark Anderson
Peter Anderson
Phil Auge
Paul Baker
Scott Baker
Doug Barnes
Scott Bauerman
Chris Bell
Tom Benzenberg
Maria Bianchi-Lastra
Jason Chai
Chi Lou Cheang
Oliver Dering
Minako Domen
Carmello Echanis
Mike Fish
Dean Flora
Jan Florendo
Kelly Forseth
Allen Frost
Rick Fuller
Teresa Funk
Rick Gagliano
Phillip Habell
Alexander Herter
Rich Holt
Steven Hong
Kyle Hughes
David Jerke
Jeff Johnson
Matt Johnson
Jean Jonas
Eric Jorgenson
Suzanne Knapp
Masatoshi Kasai
Kari Kimura
David Larsen

Jarred Lowrey
Christopher Luthi
Francesco Maccarone
Martin MacDonald
Rex Manzano
Kaoru Matsumura
Erik Mott
Glenn Newton
Titian Niosi
Homero Nishiwaki
Jeff Nye
Ken Olkonen
Todd Ottmar
Casey Pritchett
Shaun Roth
Greg Rowe
Justin James Rumpeltes
David Sanchez
Ed Sauerlinder
Cameron Schoepp
George Sharp
David Sorey
Matt Stevens
Megumi Tamanaha
Tom Trineer
Huy Thontat
Mike Torgerson
Linda Uehara
Bonnie Vesperman
Scott Wagner
Tim Walker
Todd Walker
Keenan Widrig
Carol Wilkinson
Napier Wright
Gary Yoshimura

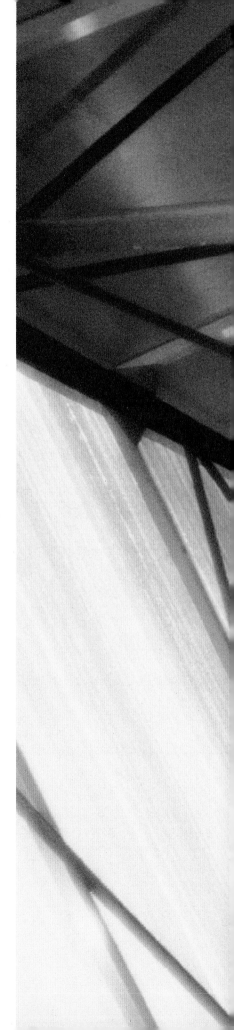

MARK ANDERSON AND PETER ANDERSON ARE PARTNERS IN THE FIRM ANDERSON ANDERSON ARCHITECTURE IN SEATTLE, WASHINGTON. THEY GREW UP IN TACOMA, WASHINGTON, AND ATTENDED PACIFIC LUTHERAN UNIVERSITY, WHERE THEIR FATHER IS A PROFESSOR OF CHEMISTRY. MARK HAS AN UNDERGRADUATE DEGREE IN MODERN ASIAN HISTORY, PETER IN FRENCH LANGUAGE AND LITERATURE. THEY RECEIVED MASTER OF ARCHITECTURE DEGREES FROM HARVARD UNIVERSITY, IN 1986 AND 1988 RESPECTIVELY, AND PETER ADDITIONALLY STUDIED UNDER OTTO PIENE AT THE CENTER FOR ADVANCED VISUAL STUDIES AT M.I.T. PETER HAS STUDIED AND WORKED IN FRANCE AND ITALY, AND MARK HAS WORKED AS A CONSTRUCTION LABORER IN GERMANY. THEY BOTH WORKED AS CARPENTERS FROM A YOUNG AGE, BEFORE STARTING THEIR OWN CONSTRUCTION COMPANY, BAY PACIFIC CONSTRUCTION, IN 1984, A FIRM THAT HAS BUILT EXTENSIVELY IN WASHINGTON STATE AND IN JAPAN. SINCE 1983 THEY HAVE COLLABORATED FREQUENTLY WITH SCULPTOR CAMERON SCHOEPP ON PUBLIC ART AND INSTALLATION PROJECTS UNDER THE GROUP NAME JET CONSTRUCTION. MARK AND PETER ANDERSON HAVE WORKED EXTENSIVELY IN ASIA, BUILDING, RESEARCHING, AND TEACHING, AND HAVE RECENTLY BEEN TEACHING AT THE UNIVERSITY OF HAWAII AT MANOA SCHOOL OF ARCHITECTURE, CONDUCTING JOINT STUDIO AND RESEARCH PROGRAMS WITH UNIVERSITIES IN ASIA.

DONLYN LYNDON IS PROFESSOR OF ARCHITECTURE AT THE UNIVERSITY OF CALIFORNIA, BERKELEY, AND HAS SERVED AS CHAIR OF THE DEPARTMENTS OF ARCHITECTURE AT BERKELEY, MASSACHUSETTS INSTITUTE OF TECHNOLOGY, AND THE UNIVERSITY OF OREGON. HE IS A PARTNER IN THE DESIGN FIRM LYNDON/BUCHANAN ASSOCIATES, EDITOR OF THE JOURNAL PLACES, AND BOARD MEMBER OF THE INTERNATIONAL LABORATORY OF ARCHITECTURE AND URBAN DESIGN (ILAUD).

CAMERON SCHOEPP IS A SCULPTOR LIVING IN FORT WORTH, TEXAS, AND IS HEAD OF THE SCULPTURE PROGRAM AT THE UNIVERSITY OF DALLAS.

ANDREW ZAGO IS COFOUNDER OF AKS RUNO ARCHITECTURE IN LOS ANGELES, AND CURRENTLY PRINCIPAL OF ZAGO ARCHITECTURE IN DETROIT, MICHIGAN.

ANNE BUSH IS A GRAPHIC DESIGNER AND HEAD OF THE DESIGN PROGRAM AT THE UNIVERSITY OF HAWAII DEPARTMENT OF ART IN HONOLULU.